# THE BATTLE OF BLENHEIM

# THE BATTLE OF BLENHEIM

## HILAIRE BELLOC

ISBN: 978-93-90387-99-1

Published:                1911

# PLATE I. THE BATTLE OF BLENHEIM.

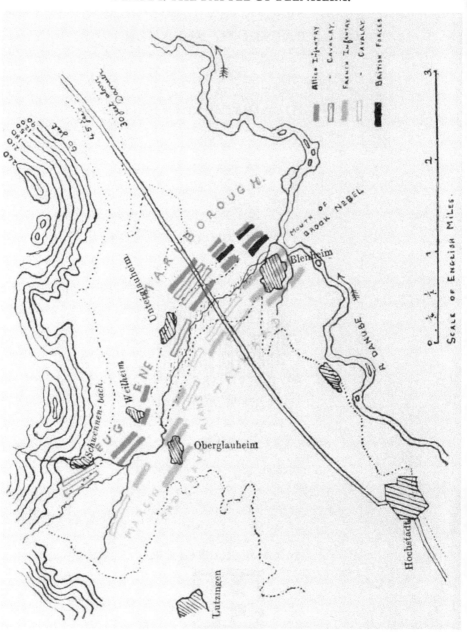

*Frontispiece.*

# THE BATTLE OF BLENHEIM

BY

HILAIRE BELLOC

1911

# CONTENTS

# LIST OF ILLUSTRATIONS

# THE BATTLE OF BLENHEIM

# PART I

## THE POLITICAL OBJECTIVE

The proper understanding of a battle and of its historical significance is only possible in connection with the campaign of which it forms a part; and the campaign can only be understood when we know the political object which it was designed to serve.

A battle is no more than an incident in a campaign. However decisive in its immediate result upon the field, its value to the general conducting it depends on its effect upon the whole of his operations, that is, upon the campaign in which he is engaged.

A campaign, again, is but the armed effort of one society to impose its will in some particular upon another society. Every such effort must have a definite political object. If this object is served the campaign is successful. If it is not served the campaign is a failure. Many a campaign which began or even concluded with a decisive action in favour of one of the two belligerents has failed because, in the result, the political object which the victory was attempting was not reached. Conversely, many a campaign, the individual actions of which were tactical defeats, terminated in favour of the defeated party, upon whom the armed effort was not sufficient to impose the will of his adversary, or to compel him to that political object which the adversary was seeking. In other words, military success can be measured only in terms of civil policy.

It is therefore essential, before approaching the study of any action, even of one so decisive and momentous as the Battle of Blenheim, to start with a general view of the political situation which brought about hostilities, and of the political object of those hostilities; only then, after grasping the measure in which the decisive action in question affected the whole campaign, can we judge how the campaign, in its turn, compassed the political end for which it was designed.

The war whose general name is that of the Spanish Succession was undertaken by certain combined powers against Louis XIV. of France (and such allies as that monarch could secure upon his side) in order to prevent the succession of his grandson to the crown of Spain.

With the various national objects which Holland, England, the Empire and certain of the German princes, as also Savoy and Portugal, may have had in view when they joined issue with the French monarch, military history is not concerned. It is enough to know that their objects, though combining them against a common foe, were not identical, and the degrees of interest with which they regarded the compulsion of Louis XIV. to forego the placing of his grandson upon the Spanish throne were very different. It is this which will largely explain the various conduct of the allies during the progress of the struggle; but all together sought the humiliation of Louis, and joined on the common ground of the Spanish Succession.

The particular object, then, of the campaign of Blenheim (and of those campaigns which immediately preceded and succeeded it) was the prevention of the unison of the crowns of France and Spain in the hands of two branches of the same family. Tested by this particular issue alone, the campaign of Blenheim, and the whole series of campaigns to which it belongs, failed. Louis XIV. maintained his grandson upon the throne of Spain; and the issue of the long war could not impose upon him the immediate political object of the allies.

But there was a much larger and more general object engaged, which was no less than the defence of Austria—more properly the Empire—and of certain minor States, against what had grown to be the overwhelming power of the French monarchy.

From this standpoint the whole period of Louis XIV.'s reign—all the last generation of the seventeenth century and the first decade and more of the eighteenth—may be regarded as a struggle between the soldiers of Louis XIV. (and their allies) upon the one hand, and Austria, with certain minor powers concerned in the defence of their independence or integrity, upon the other.

In this struggle Great Britain was neutral or benevolent in its sympathies in so far as those sympathies were Stuart; but all that part of English public life called *Whig*, all the group of English aristocrats who desired the abasement of the Crown, perhaps the mass of the nation also, was opposed, both in its interests and in its opinions, to the supremacy of Louis XIV. upon the Continent.

William of Orange, who had been called to the English throne by the Revolution of 1688, was the most determined opponent Louis had in Europe. Apart from him, the general interests of the London merchants, and the commercial interests of the nation as a whole, were in antagonism to the claims of the Bourbon monarchy. We therefore find the forces of Great Britain, in men, ships, guns, and money, arrayed against Louis throughout the end of his reign, and especially during this last great war.

Now, from this general standpoint—by far the most important—the war of the Spanish Succession is but part of the general struggle against Louis XIV.; and in that general struggle the campaign of 1704, and the battle of Blenheim which was its climax, are at once of the highest historical importance, and a singular example of military success.

For if the general political object be considered, which was the stemming of the French tide of victory and the checking of the Bourbon power, rather than the particular matter of the succession of the Spanish throne, then it was undoubtedly the campaign of 1704 which turned the tide; and Blenheim must always be remembered in history as the great defeat from which dates the retreat of the military power of the French in that epoch, and the gradual beating back of Louis XIV.'s forces to those frontiers which may be regarded as the natural boundaries of France.

Not all the French conquests were lost, nor by any means was the whole great effort of the reign destroyed. But the peril which the military aptitude of the French under so great a man as Louis XIV. presented to the minor States of Europe and to the Austrian empire was definitely checked when the campaign of Blenheim was brought to its successful conclusion. That battle was the first of the great defeats which exhausted the resources of Louis, put him, for the first time in his long reign, upon a close defensive, and restored the European balance which his years of unquestioned international power had disturbed.

Blenheim, then, may justly rank among the decisive actions of European history.

In connection with the campaign of which it formed a part, it gave to that campaign all its meaning and all its complete success.

In connection with the general struggle against Louis, that campaign formed the turning point between the flow and the ebb in the stream of military power which Louis XIV. commanded and had set in motion.

From the day of Blenheim, August 13th, 1704, onwards, the whole French effort was for seven years a desperate losing game, which, if its end was saved from disaster by the high statesmanship of the king and the devotion of his people, was none the less the ruin of that ambitious policy which had coincided with the great days of Versailles.

The war was conducted, as I have said, by various allies. Its success depended, therefore, upon various commanders regarded as coequal, acting as colleagues rather than as principals and subordinates. But the story of the great march to the Danube and its harvest at Blenheim, which we are about to review, sufficiently proves that the deciding genius in the whole affair was that of John Churchill, Duke of Marlborough. The plan was indeed Eugene's; and in the battle itself he shared the glory with his English friend and colleague. Again, the British troops present were few indeed compared with the total of the allied forces. At Blenheim, in particular, they amounted to less than a third of the numbers present. The excellence of their material, however, their magnificent work at the Schellenberg and on Blenheim field itself, coupled with the fact that the general to whom the final success is chiefly due was the great military genius of this country, warrants the historian in classing this battle among British actions, and in treating its story as a national affair.

I will approach the story of the campaign and of the battle by a conspectus of the field of war in which Marlborough was so unexpectedly to show the military genius which remains his single title to respect and his chief claim to renown.

# PART II

## THE EARLY WAR

In order to grasp the strategic problem presented to Marlborough and the allies in the spring of 1704, it is first necessary to understand the diplomatic position at the outbreak of the war, and the military disposition of the two years 1702 and 1703, and thus the general position of the armies which preceded Marlborough's march to the Danube.

Louis XIV. recognised his grandson as king of Spain late in 1700. The coalition immediately formed against him was at first imperfect. Savoy, with its command of the passes over the Alps into Austrian territory, was in Louis' favour. England, whose support of his enemies was (for reasons to be described) a capital factor in the issue, had not yet joined those enemies. But, from several causes, among the chief of which was Louis' recognition of the Pretender as king of England after James the II.'s death, the opinion of the English aristocracy, and perhaps of the English people, was fixed, and in the last months of 1701 the weight of England was thrown into the balance against France.

Why have I called this—the decision of the English Parliament—a capital factor in the issue of the war?

Excepting for a moment the military genius of Marlborough—whose great capacity had not yet been tested in so large a field—two prime characters gave to Great Britain a deciding voice in what was to follow. The first of these was her wealth, the second that aristocratic constitution of her polity which was now definitely established, and which, for nearly a century and a half, was to make her strength unique in its quality among all the elements of European competition.

As to the first of these—the *Wealth* of England—it is a matter of such importance to the comprehension of all the eighteenth century and most of the nineteenth that it should merit a far longer analysis and affirmation than can be devoted to it in these few lines. It must be enough for our purpose to say that Great Britain, from about 1680 onwards, was not only wealthier (in proportion to her population) than the powers with whom she had to deal as enemies or allies, but was also proceeding to increase that wealth at a rate far exceeding that of her rivals. Again, what was perhaps, for the purposes of war, the chief point of all, England held that wealth in a mobile, fluid form, which could at once be translated into munitions, the wages of mercenaries, or the hire of transports, within the shortest time, and at almost any point in Western and Northern Europe.

Essentially commercial, already possessed of a solid line of enterprises beyond the seas, having defeated and passed the Dutch in the race for mercantile supremacy, England could afford or withhold at her choice the most valuable and rapid form of support—money.

How true this was, even those in Europe who had not appreciated the changed conditions of Great Britain immediately perceived when the determination of Parliament, at the end of 1701, to support the alliance against Louis XIV., took the form of voting 40,000 men, all of whom would be immediately supplied and paid with English money.

True, of the 40,000 not half were British; but (save for the excellent quality of the British troops), the point was more or less indifferent. The important thing was that England was able to provide and to maintain this immense accretion to the coalition against France, and to use it where she would. We shall see later how this power turned the fate of the war.

If I have insisted so strongly upon the financial factor, it is both because that factor is misappreciated in most purely military histories, and also because, in the changed circumstances of our own time, it is not easy for the reader to take for granted, as did his ancestors, the overwhelming superiority which England once enjoyed in mobilised wealth, usable after this kind. It can best be compared to the similar superiority enjoyed in the Middle Ages by the Republic of Venice, to whose fortunes, both good and ill, the story of modern England affords so strange a parallel.

The second factor I have mentioned—the aristocratic constitution of the country—though almost equally important, is somewhat more elusive, and might be more properly challenged by a critic.

England had not, in the first years of the eighteenth century, reached that calm and undisturbed solidity which is the mark of an aristocratic State at its zenith. Faction was bitter, the opposition between the old loyalty to the Crown and the new national régime was so determined as to make civil war possible at any moment. This condition of affairs was to last for a generation, and it was not until the middle of the eighteenth century was passed that it disappeared.

Nevertheless, compared with the Continental States, Great Britain already presented by 1701 that elasticity in substance and tenacity in policy which accompany aristocratic institutions. Corruption might be rife, but it was already growing difficult to purchase the services of a member of the governing class against the national interests. That knowledge of public affairs, diffused throughout a small and closely combined social class, which is the mark of an aristocracy, was already apparent. The power of choosing, from a narrow and well-known field, the best talents for any particular office (which is another mark of aristocracy), was already a power apparent in the government of this country. The solidity which, in the face of a common enemy, an aristocracy always displays, the long-livedness, as of a corporate body, which an aristocracy enjoys, and which permits it to follow with such strict continuity whatever line of foreign policy it has undertaken, was clearly defining itself at the moment of which I write.

In a word, the new settlement of English life upon the basis of class government, the exclusion of the mass of the people from public affairs, the decay (if you will) of a lively public opinion, the presence of that hopeless disinherited class which now forms the majority of our industrial population; the organisation of the universities, of justice, of the legislature, of the executive, as parts of one social class; the close grasp which that class now had upon the land and capital of the whole country, which it could utilise immediately for interior development or for a war — all this marked the youth and vigour of an oligarchic England, which was for so long to be at once invulnerable and impregnable.

At what expense in morals, and therefore in ultimate strength and happiness, such experiments are played, is no matter for discussion in a military history. We must be content to remark what vigour her new constitution gave to the efforts of England in the field, while yet that constitution was young.

England, then, having thrown this great weight into the scale of the Empire, and against France, the campaign of 1702 was entered upon with the chances in favour of the former, and with the latter in an anxiety very different from the pride which Louis XIV. had taken for granted in the early part of his reign.

If the reader will consider the map of Western Europe, the effect of England's joining the allies will be apparent.

The frontier between the Spanish Netherlands and Holland — that is, between modern Belgium and Holland — was the frontier between the forces of Louis XIV. and those of opponents upon the north. Thus Antwerp and Ostend were in the hands of the Bourbon, for the Spanish Netherlands had passed into the hands of the French king's grandson, and the French and Spanish forces were combined. Further east, towards the Upper Rhine, a French force lay in the district of Cleves, and all the fortresses on the Meuse, running in a line south of that post, with the exception of Maestricht, were in French hands.

French armies held or threatened the Middle Rhine. Upon the Upper Rhine and upon the Danube an element of the highest moment in favour of France had appeared when the Elector of Bavaria had declared for Louis XIV., and against Austria.

Had not England intervened with the great weight of gold and that considerable contingent of men (in all, eighteen of the new forty thousand), France would have easily held her northern position upon the frontier of Holland and the Lower Rhine, while the Elector of Bavaria, joining forces with the French army upon the Upper Rhine, would have marched upon Vienna.

The Emperor was harried by the rising of the Hungarians behind him; and as the principal forces of the French king would not have been detained in the north, the whole weight of France, combined with her new ally the Elector of Bavaria, would have been thrown upon the Upper Danube.

As it was, this plan was, in its inception at least, partially successful, but only in its inception, and only partially.

For, with the summer of 1702, Marlborough, though hampered by the fears of the Dutch with whom he had to act in concert, cleared the French out of Cleves, caused them to retire southward in the face of the great accession of strength which he brought with the new troops in English pay and the English contingents. Following the French retirement, he swept the whole valley of the Meuse,[1] and took its fastnesses from Liége downwards, all along the course of the stream.

By the end of the year this northern front of the French armies was imperilled, and Marlborough and his allies in that part hoped to undertake with the next season the reduction of the Spanish Netherlands.

It must be remembered, in connection with this plan, that France has always been nervous with regard to her north-eastern frontier; that the loss of this frontier leaves a way open to Paris: an advance from Belgium was to the French monarchy what an advance along the Danube was to Austria—the prime peril of all. As yet, France was nowhere near grave peril in this quarter, but pressure there marred her general plans upon the Danube.

Nevertheless, the march upon Vienna by the Upper Danube had been prepared with some success. While part of the northern frontier was thus being pressed and part menaced, while the Meuse was being cleared of French garrisons, and the French fortresses on it taken by Marlborough and his allies, the Elector of Bavaria had seized Ulm. The French upon the Upper Rhine, under Villars, defeated the Prince of Baden at Friedlingen, and established a road through the New Forest by which Louis XIV.'s forces, combined with those of the Elector of Bavaria, could advance eastward upon the Emperor's capital. It was designed that in the next year, 1703, the troops of Savoy, in alliance with those of France, should march from North Italy through the passes of the Alps and the Tyrol upon Vienna, while at the same time the Franco-Bavarian forces should march down the Danube towards the same objective.

When the campaign of 1703 opened, however, two unexpected events determined what was to follow.

The first was the failure of Marlborough in the north to take Antwerp, and in general his inability to press France further at that point; the second, the defection of Savoy from the French alliance.

As to the first—Marlborough's failure against Antwerp. The Spanish Netherlands were now solidly held; the forces of the allies were indeed increasing perpetually in this neighbourhood, but it appeared as though the attempt to reduce Brabant, Hainault, and Flanders, which are here the bulwark of France, would be tedious, and perhaps barren. A sort of "consolation" advance was indeed made upon the Rhine, and Bonn was captured; but no more was done in this quarter.

As to the second point, the solid occupation of the Upper Danube by the Franco-Bavarians was indeed fully accomplished. The imperial forces were defeated upon the bank of that river at Hochstadt, but the advance upon Vienna failed, for the second half of the plan, the march from Northern Italy upon Austria, through the Tyrol, had come to nothing, through the defection of Savoy. The turning of the scale against Louis by the action of England was beginning to have its effect;

[1] It was this success which to Marlborough's existing earldom added the high dignity of Duke, by letters patent of December 16, 1702.

Portugal had already joined the coalition, and now Savoy had refused to continue her help of the Bourbons.

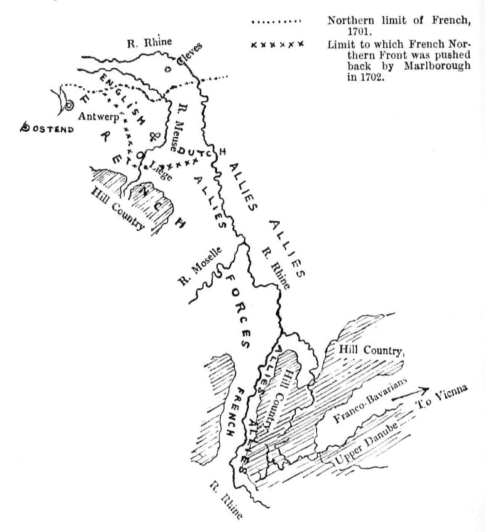

| | |
|---|---|
| ·········· | Northern limit of French, 1701. |
| ✕✕✕✕✕ | Limit to which French Northern Front was pushed back by Marlborough in 1702. |

**The General Situation in 1703.**

The year 1704 opened, therefore, with this double situation: to the south Austria had been saved for the moment, but was open to immediate attack in the campaign to come; meanwhile, the French had proved so solidly seated in the Spanish Netherlands (or Belgium) that repeated attacks on them in this quarter would in all probability prove barren.

It was under these circumstances that Eugene of Savoy came to the great decision which marked the year of Blenheim. He determined that it was best—if he could persuade his colleagues—to carry the war into that territory which was particularly menaced. He conceived the plan of marching a great force from the

Netherlands right down to the field of the Upper Danube. There could be checked the proposed march upon the heart of the coalition, which was Vienna. There, if fortune served the allies, they would by victory make all further chance of marching a Franco-Bavarian force down the Danube impossible; meanwhile, and at any rate, the new step would alarm all French effort towards the Upper Rhine, weaken the French organisation upon its northern frontier, and so permit of a return of the allies to an attack there at a later time.

Eugene of Savoy was a member of the cadet branch of that royal house. His grandfather, the younger son of Charles Emmanuel, had founded the family called Savoy Carignan. His father had been married to one of Mazarin's nieces. Eugene was her fifth son, and at this moment not quite forty years of age.

His character, motives, and genius must be clearly seized if we are to appreciate the campaign and the battle of Blenheim.

It was the Italian blood which formed that character most, but he was thoroughly French by birth and training. Born in Paris, and desiring a career in the French army, it was a slight offered to his mother by the French king that gave his whole life a personal hatred of Louis XIV. for its motive. From boyhood till his death, between sixty and seventy, this great captain directed his energies uniquely against the fortunes of the French king. When, later in life, there was an attempt to acquire his talents for the French service, he replied that he hoped to re-enter France, but only as an invader. It has been complained that he lacked precision in detail, and that as an organiser he was somewhat at fault; but he had no equal for rapidity of vision, and for seizing the essential point in a strategic problem. From that day in his twentieth year when he had assisted at Sobiesky's destruction of the Turks before Vienna, through his own great victory which crushed that same enemy somewhat later at Zenta, in all his career this quality of immediate perception had been supremely apparent.

He was at this moment—the end of the campaign of 1703—the head of the imperial council of war; and he it was who first grasped the strategic necessity which 1703 had created. The determination to carry the defence of the empire into the valley of the Upper Danube was wholly his own. He wrote to Marlborough suggesting a withdrawal of forces as considerable as possible from the northern field to the southern.

By a happy accident, the judgment of the Englishman exactly coincided with his own, and indeed there was so precise a sympathy between these two very different men that when they met in the course of the ensuing campaign there sprang up between them not only a lasting friendship, but a mutual comprehension which made the combination of their talents invincible during those half dozen years of the war which all but destroyed the French power.

Such was the origin of Marlborough's advance southward from the Netherlands in the early summer of 1704, an advance famous in history under the title of "the march to the Danube."

# PART III
## THE MARCH TO THE DANUBE

The position of the enemy at the moment when Marlborough's march to the Danube from the Netherlands was conceived may be observed in the sketch map on page 21.

Under Villeroy, who must be regarded as the chief of the French commanders of the moment, lay the principal army of Louis XIV., with the duty of defending the northern front and of watching the Lower Rhine.

It was this main force which was expected to have to meet the attack of Marlborough and the Dutch in the same field of operations as had seen the troops in English pay at work during the two preceding years. But Villeroy was, of course, free to detach troops southwards somewhat towards the Middle Rhine, or the valley of the Moselle, if, as later seemed likely, an attack should be made in that direction.

On the Upper Rhine, and in Alsace generally, lay Tallard with his corps. This marshal had captured certain crossing-places over the Rhine, but had all his munitions and the mass of his strength permanently on the left bank.

Finally, Marcin, with his French contingent, and Max-Emanuel, the Elector of Bavaria, with the Bavarian army, held the whole of the Upper Danube, from Ulm right down to and past the Austrian frontier.

Over against these forces of the French and their Bavarian allies we must set, first, the Dutch forces in the north, including the garrisons of the towns on the Meuse which Marlborough had conquered and occupied; and, in the same field, the forces in the pay of England (including the English contingents). These amounted in early 1704 to 50,000 men, which Marlborough was to command.

Next, upon the Middle Rhine, and watching Tallard in Alsace, was Prince Eugene, who had been summoned from Hungary by the Imperial government to defend this bulwark of Germany, but his army was small compared to the forces in the north.

Finally, the Margrave of Baden, Louis, with another separate army, was free to act at will in Upper Germany, to occupy posts in the Black Forest, or to retire eastward into the heart of Germany or towards the Danube as circumstances might dictate. This force was also small. It was supplemented by local militia raised to defend particular passes in the Black Forest, and these, again, were supported by the armed peasantry.

It is essential to a comprehension of the whole scheme to understand that *before* the march to the Danube the whole weight of the alliance against the French lay in the north, upon the frontier of Holland, the valley of the Meuse, and the Lower Rhine. The successes of Bavaria in the previous year had given the Bavarian army, with its French contingent, a firm grip upon the Upper Danube, and the possibility of marching upon Vienna itself when the campaign of 1704 should open.

The great march upon the Danube which Eugene had conceived, and which Marlborough was to execute so triumphantly, was a plan to withdraw the weight of the allied forces suddenly from the north to the south; to transfer the main weapon acting against France from the Netherlands to Bavaria itself; to do this so rapidly and with so little leakage of information to the enemy as would prevent his heading off the advance by a parallel and faster movement upon his part, or his strengthening his forces upon the Danube before Marlborough's should reach that river.

Such was the scheme of the march to the Danube which we are now about to follow; but before undertaking a description of the great and successful enterprise, the reader must permit me a word of distinction between a strategic move and that tactical accident which we call a battle. In the absence of such a distinction, the campaign of Blenheim and the battle which gives it its name would be wholly misread.

A great battle, especially if it be of a decisive character, not only changes history, but has a dramatic quality about it which fixes the attention of mankind.

The general reader, therefore, tends to regard the general movements of a campaign as mere preliminaries to, or explanations of, the decisive action which may conclude it.

This is particularly the case with the readers attached to the victorious side. The French layman, in the days before universal service in France, wrote and read his history of 1805 as though the march of the Grand Army were deliberately intended to conclude with Austerlitz. The English reader and writer still tends to read and write of Marlborough's march to the Danube as though it were aimed at the field of Blenheim.

This error or illusion is part of that general deception so common to historical study which has been well called "reading history backwards." We know the event; to the actors in it the future was veiled. Our knowledge of what is to come colours and distorts our judgment of the motive and design of a general.

The march to the Danube was, like all strategic movements, a general plan animated by a general objective. It was not a particular thrust at a particular point, destined to achieve a highly particular result at that point.

Armies are moved with the object of imposing political changes upon an opponent. If that opponent accepts these changes, not necessarily after a pitched battle, but in any other fashion, the strategical object of the march is achieved.

Though the march conclude in a defeat, it may be strategically sound; though it conclude in a victory, it may be strategically unsound. Napoleon's march into

Russia in 1812 was strategically sound. Had Russia risked a great battle and lost it, the historical illusion of which I speak would treat the campaign as a designed preface to the battle. Had Russia risked such a battle and been successful, the historical illusion of which I speak would call the strategy of the advance faulty.

As we know, the advance failed partly through the weather, partly through the spirit of the Russian people, not through a general action. But in conception and in execution the strategy of Napoleon in that disastrous year was just as excellent as though the great march had terminated not in disaster but in success.

Similarly, the reputation justly earned by Marlborough when he brought his troops from the Rhine to the Danube must be kept distinct from his tactical successes in the field at the conclusion of the effort. He was to run a grave risk at Donauwörth, he was to blunder badly in attacking the village of Blenheim, he was to be in grave peril even in the last phase of the battle, when Eugene just saved the centre with his cavalry.

Had chance, which is the major element in equal combats, foiled him at Donauwörth or broken his attempt at Blenheim, the march to the Danube would still remain a great thing in history. Had Tallard refused battle on that day, as he certainly should have done, the march to the Danube would still deserve its great place in the military records of Europe.

When we have seized the fact that Marlborough's great march was but a general strategic movement of which the action at Blenheim was the happy but accidental close, we must next remark that the advance to the Danube was the more meritorious, and gives the higher lustre to Marlborough's fame as a general, from the fact that it was an attempt involving a great military hazard, and that yet that attempt had to be made in the face of political difficulties of peculiar severity.

In other words, Marlborough was handicapped in a fashion which lends his success a character peculiar to itself, and worthy of an especial place in history.

This handicap may be stated by a consideration of three points which cover its whole character.

The first of these points concerns the physical conditions of the move; the other two are peculiar to the political differences of the allies.

It was in the nature of the move that a high hazard was involved in it. The general had calculated, as a general always must, the psychology of his opponent. If he were wrong in his calculation, the advance on the Danube could but lead to disaster. It was for him to judge whether the French were so nervous about the centre of their position upon the Rhine as to make them cling to it to the last moment, and tend to believe that it was either along the Moselle or (when he had left that behind) in Alsace that he intended to attack. In other words, it was for him to make the French a little too late in changing their dispositions, a little too late in discovering what his real plan was, and therefore a little too late in massing larger reinforcements upon the Upper Danube, where he designed to be before them.

Marlborough guessed his opponent's psychology rightly; the French marshals hesitated just too long, their necessity of communicating with Louis at Versailles further delayed them, and the great hazard which he risked was therefore risked with judgment. But a hazard it remained until almost the last days of its fruition. The march must be rapid; it involved a thousand details, each requiring his supervision and his exact calculation, his knowledge of what could be expected of his troops, and his survey of daily supply.

There was another element of hazard.

Arrived at his destination upon the plains of the Danube, Marlborough would be very far from any good base of supply.

The country lying in the triangle between the Upper Danube and the Middle Rhine, especially that part of it which is within striking distance of the Danube, is mountainous and ill provided with those large towns, that mobilisable wealth, and those stores of vehicles, munitions, food, and remounts which are the indispensable sustenance of an army.

The industry of modern Germany has largely transformed this area, but even to-day it is one in which good depots would be rare to find. Two hundred years ago, the tangle of hills was far more deserted and far worse provided.

By the time Marlborough should have effected his junction with his ally in the upper valley of the Danube only two bases of supply would be within any useful distance of the new and distant place to which he was transferring his great force.

The most important of these, his chief base, and his only principal store of munitions and every other requisite, was *Nuremberg*; and that town was a good week from the plains upon the bank of the Danube where he proposed to act. As an advanced base nearer to the river, he could only count upon the lesser town of *Nordlingen*.

Therefore, even if he should successfully reach the field of action which he proposed, cross the hills between the two river basins without loss or delay, and be ready to act as he hoped upon the banks of the Danube before the end of June, his stay could not be indefinitely prolonged there, and his every movement would be undertaken under the anxiety which must ever haunt a commander dependent on an insufficient or too distant base of supply. This anxiety, be it noted, would rapidly increase with every march he might have to take southward of the Danube, and with every day's advance into Bavaria itself, if, as he hoped, the possibility of such an advance should crown his efforts.

We have seen that the great hazard which Marlborough risked made it necessary, as he advanced southward up the Rhine during the first half of his march, to keep Villeroy and Tallard doubtful as to whether his objective was the Moselle or, later, Alsace; and while they were still in suspense, abruptly to leave the valley of the Rhine and make for the crossing of the hills towards the Danube. So long as the French marshals remained uncertain of his intentions, they would not dare to detach any very large body of troops from the Rhine valley to the Elector's aid: under the conditions of the time, the clever handling of movement and information might create a gap of a week at least between his first divergence from the Rhine and his enemy's full appreciation that he was heading for the south-east.

He so concealed his information and so ordered his baffling movements as to achieve that end.

So much for the general hazard which would have applied to any commander undertaking such an advance.

But, as I have said, there were two other points peculiar to Marlborough's political position.

The first was, that he was not wholly free to act, as, for instance, Cæsar in Gaul was free, or Napoleon after 1799. He must perpetually arrange matters, in the first stages with the Dutch commissioner, later with the imperial general, Prince Louis of Baden, who was his equal in command. He must persuade and even trick certain of his allies in all the first steps of the great business; he must accommodate himself to others throughout the whole of it.

Secondly, the direction in which he took himself separated him from the possibility of rapidly communicating his designs, his necessities, his chances, or his perils to what may be called his *moral* base. This moral base, the seat both of his own Government and of the Dutch (his principal concern), lay, of course, near the North Sea, and under the immediate supervision of England and the Hague. This is a point which the modern reader may be inclined to ridicule until he remembers under what conditions the shortest message, let alone detailed plans and the execution of considerable orders, could alone be performed two hundred years ago. By a few bad roads, across a veritable dissected map of little independent or quasi-independent polities, each with its own frontier and prejudices and independent government, the messenger (often a single messenger) must pass through a space of time equivalent to the passage of a continent to-day, and through risks and difficulties such as would to-day be wholly eliminated by the telegraph. The messenger was further encumbered by every sort of change from town to town, in local opinion, and the opportunities for aid.

More than this, in marching to the Danube, Marlborough was putting between himself and that upon which he morally, and most of all upon which he physically, relied, a barrier of difficult mountain land.

Having mentioned this barrier, it is the place for me to describe the physical conditions of that piece of strategy, and I will beg the reader to pay particular attention to the accompanying map, and to read what follows closely in connection with it.

In all war, strategy considers routes, and routes are determined by obstacles.

Had the world one flat and uniform surface, the main problems of strategy would not exist.

The surface of the world is diversified by certain features — rivers, chains of hills, deserts, marshes, seas, etc. — the passage across which presents difficulties peculiar to an army, and it is essential to the reading of military history to appreciate these difficulties; for the degrees of impediment which natural features present to thousands upon the march are utterly different from those which they present to individuals or to civilian parties in time of peace. Since it is to difficulties of this latter sort that we are most accustomed by our experience, the student of a campaign will often ask himself (if he is new to his subject) why such and such an apparently insignificant stream or narrow river, such and such a range of hills over which he has walked on some holiday without the least embarrassment, have been treated by the great captains as obstacles of the first moment.

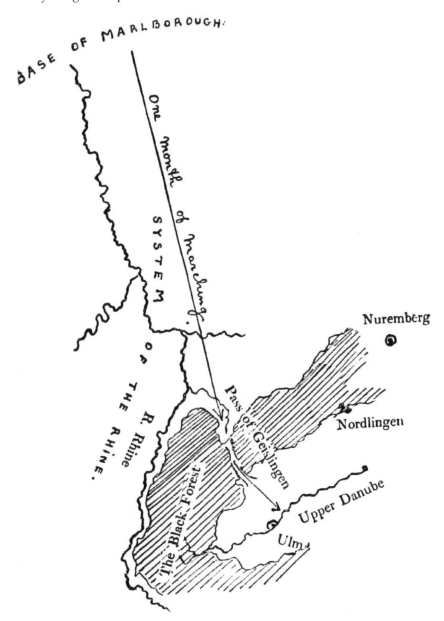

Map showing the peril of Marlborough's march to the Danube, beyond the hills which separate the Rhine from the Danube.

The reason that obstacles of any sort present the difficulty they do to an army, and present it in the high degree which military history discovers, is twofold.

First, an army consists in a great body of human beings, artificially gathered together under conditions which do not permit of men supplying their own wants by agriculture or other forms of labour. They are gathered together for the principal purpose of fighting. They must be fed; they must be provided with ammunition, usually with shelter and with firing, and if possible with remounts for their cavalry; reinforcements for every branch of their service must be able to reach them along known and friendly (or well-defended) roads, called their *lines of communication*. These must proceed from some *base*, that is from some secure place in which stores of men and material can be accumulated.

Next, it is important to notice that variations in speed between two opposed forces will nearly always put the slow at a disadvantage in the face of the more prompt. For just as in boxing the quicker man can stop one blow and get another in where the slower man would fail, or just as in football the faster runner can head off the man with the ball, so in war superior mobility is a fixed factor of advantage—but a factor far more serious than it is in any game. The force which moves most quickly can "walk round" its opponent, can choose its field for action, can strike in flank, can escape, can effect a junction where the slower force would fail.

It is these two causes, then—the artificial character of an army, with its vast numbers collected in one place and dependent for existence upon the labour of others and the supreme importance of rapidity—which between them render obstacles that seem indifferent to a civilian in time of peace so formidable to a General upon the march.

The heavy train, the artillery, the provisioning of the force, can in general only proceed upon good ways or by navigable rivers. At any rate, if the army departs from these, a rival army in possession of such means of progress will have the supreme advantage of mobility.

Again, upon the flat an army may proceed by many parallel roads, and thus in a number of comparatively short columns, marching upon one front towards a common rendezvous. But in hilly country it will be confined to certain defiles, sometimes very few, often reduced to *one* practicable pass. There is no possibility of an advance by many routes in short columns, each in touch with its neighbours; the whole advance resolves itself into one interminable file.

Now, in proportion to the length of a column, the units of which must each march one directly behind the other, do the mechanical difficulties of conducting such a column increase. Every accident or shock in the long line is aggravated in proportion to the length of the line. Finally, a force thus drawn out on the march in one exiguous and lengthy trail is in the worst possible disposition for meeting an attack delivered upon it from either side.

All this, which is true of the actual march of the army, is equally true of its power to maintain its supply over a line of hills (to take that example of an obstacle); and therefore a line of hills, especially if these hills be confused and steep, and especially if they be provided with but bad roads across them, will dangerously isolate an army whose general base lies upon the further side of them.

What the reader has just read explains the peculiar character which the valley of the Upper Danube has always had in the history of Western European war.

The Rhine and its tributaries form one great system of communications, diversified, indeed, by many local accidents of hill and marsh and forest, with which, for the purposes of this study, we need not concern ourselves.

In a lesser degree, the upper valley of the Danube and its tributaries, though these are largely in the nature of mountain torrents, forms another system of communications, nourishing considerable towns, drawing upon which communications, and relying upon which towns as centres of supply, an army may manœuvre.

But between the system of the Rhine and that of the Danube there runs a long sweep of very broken country, the Black Forest merging into the Swabian Jura, which in a military sense cuts off the one basin from the other.

At the opening of the eighteenth century, when that great stretch of hills had but a score of roads, none of them well kept up, when no town of any importance could be found in their valleys, and when no communication, even of a verbal message, could proceed faster than a mounted man, this sweep of hills was a very formidable obstacle indeed.

It was these hills, when Marlborough determined to strike across them, and to engage himself in the valley of the Upper Danube, which formed the chief physical factor of his hazard; for, once engaged in them, still more when he had crossed them, his appeals for aid, his reception of advice, perhaps eventually a reinforcement of men or supplies, must depend upon the Rhine valley.

True he had, the one within a week of the Danube, the other within two days of it, the couple of depots mentioned above, the principal one at Nuremberg, the advanced one at Nordlingen. Nevertheless, so long as he was upon the further or eastern side of the hills, his position would remain one of great risk, unless, indeed, or until, he had had the good fortune to destroy the forces of the enemy.

All this being before the reader, the progress of the great march may now be briefly described.

In the winter between 1703 and 1704 domestic irritation and home intrigues, with which we are not here concerned, almost persuaded Marlborough to give up his great rôle upon the Continent of Europe.

Luckily for the alliance against Louis and for the history of British arms, he returned upon this determination or phantasy, and with the very beginning of the year began his plans for the coming campaign.

He crossed first to Holland in the middle of January 1704, persuaded the Dutch Government to grant a subsidy to the German troops in the South, pretended (since he knew how nervous the Dutch would be if they heard of the plan for withdrawing a great army from their frontiers to the Danube) that he intended operating upon the Moselle, returned to England, saw with the utmost activity to the raising of recruits and to the domestic organisation of the expedition, and reached Holland again to undertake the most famous action of his life in the latter part of April.

It was upon the 5th of May that he left the Hague. He was at Maestricht till the 14th, superintending every detail and ordering the construction of bridges over the Meuse by which the advance was to begin. Upon the 16th he left by the southward road for Bedburg, and immediately his army broke winter quarters for the great march.

It was upon the 18th of May that the British regiments marched out of Ruremonde by the bridges constructed over the Meuse, aiming for the rendezvous at Bedburg.

The very beginning of the march was disturbed by the fears of the Dutch and of others, though Marlborough had carefully kept secret the design of marching to the Danube, and though all imagined that the valley of the Moselle was his objective.

Marlborough quieted these fears, and was in a better position to insist from the fact that he claimed control over the very large force which was directly in the pay of England.

He struck for the Rhine, up the valley of which he would receive further contingents, supplied by the minor members of the Grand Alliance, as he marched.

By the 23rd he was at Bonn with the cavalry, his brother Churchill following with the infantry. Thence the heavy baggage and the artillery proceeded by water up the river to Coblentz, and when Coblentz was reached (upon the 25th of May) it was apparent that the Moselle at least was not his objective, for on the next day, the 26th, he crossed both that river and the Rhine with his army, and continued his march up the right bank of the Rhine.

But this did not mean that he might not still intend to carry the war into Alsace. He was at Cassel, opposite Mayence, three days after leaving Coblentz; four days later the head of the column had reached the Neckar at Ladenberg, where bridges had already been built by Marlborough's orders, and upon the 3rd of June the troops crossed over to the further bank.

Here was the decisive junction where Marlborough must show his hand: the first few miles of his progress south-eastward across the bend of the Neckar would make it clear that his object was not Alsace, but the Danube.

He had announced to the Dutch and all Europe an attack upon the valley of the Moselle; that this was a ruse all could see when he passed Coblentz without turning up the valley of that river. The whole week following, and until he reached the Neckar, it might still be imagined that he meditated an attack upon Alsace, for he was still following the course of the Rhine. Once he diverged from the valley of this river and struck across the bend of the Neckar to the south and east, the alternative he had chosen of making the Upper Danube the seat of war was apparent.

It is therefore at this point in his advance that we must consider the art by which he had put the enemy in suspense, and confused their judgment of his design.

The first point in the problem for a modern reader to appreciate is the average rate at which news would travel at that time and in that place. A very important dispatch could cover a hundred miles and more in the day with special organisation for its delivery, and with the certitude that it had gone from one particular place to another particular place. But general daily information as to the movements of a moving enemy could not be so organised.

We must take it that the French commanders upon the left bank of the Rhine at Landau, or upon the Meuse (where Villeroy was when Marlborough began his march), would require full forty-eight hours to be informed of the objective of each new move.

For instance, on the 25th of May Marlborough's forces were approaching Coblentz. To find out what they were going to do next, the French would have to know whether they were beginning to turn up the valley of the Moselle, which begins at Coblentz, or to cross that river and be going on further south. A messenger might have been certain that the latter was their intention by midday of the 26th, but Tallard, right away on the Upper Rhine, would hardly have known this before the morning of the 29th, and by the morning of the 29th Marlborough was already opposite Mayence.

It is this gap of from one to three days in the passage of information which is so difficult for a modern man to seize, and which yet made possible all Marlborough's manœuvres to confuse the French.

Villeroy was bound to watch until, at least, the 29th of May for the chance of a campaign upon the Moselle.

Meanwhile, Tallard was not only far off in the valley of the Upper Rhine, but occupied in a remarkable operation which, had he not subsequently suffered defeat at Blenheim, would have left him a high reputation as a general.

This operation was the reinforcement of the army under the Elector of Bavaria and Marcin by a dash right through the enemy's country in the Black Forest.

Early in May the Elector of Bavaria had urgently demanded reinforcements of the French king.

The mountains between the Bavarian army and the French were held by the enemy, but the Elector hurried westward along the Danube, while Tallard, with exact synchrony and despatch, hurried eastward; each held out a hand to the other, as it were, for a rapid touch; the business of Tallard was to hand over the new troops and provisions at one exact moment, the business of the Elector was to catch the junction exactly. If it succeeded it was to be followed by a sharp retreat of either party, the one back upon the Danube eastward for his life, the other back westward upon the Rhine.

Tallard had crossed the Rhine on the 13th of May with a huge convoy of provisionment and over 7000 newly recruited troops. Within a week the thing was done. He had handed over in the nick of time the whole mass of men and things to the Elector.[2] He had done this in the midst of the Black Forest and in the heart of the enemy's country, and he immediately began his retirement upon the Rhine. Tallard was thus particularly delayed in receiving daily information of Marlborough's march.

Let us take a typical date.

On the 29th of May Tallard, retiring from the dash to help Bavaria, was still at Altenheim, on the German bank of the Rhine. It was only on that day that he learnt from Villeroy that Marlborough had no idea of marching up the Moselle, but had gone on up the Rhine towards Mayence. Marlborough had crossed the Moselle and the Rhine on the 26th, but it took Tallard three days to know it. Tallard, knowing this, would not know whether Marlborough might not still be thinking of attacking Alsace: to make that alternative loom large in the mind of the French commanders, Marlborough had had bridges prepared in front of his advance at Philipsburg—though he had, of course, no intention at all of going as far up as Philipsburg.

It was on June 3rd, as we have seen, that the foremost of Marlborough's forces were nearing the banks of the Neckar, and upon the 4th that anyone observing his troops would have clearly seen for the first time that they were striking for the Danube. But it was twenty-four hours before Tallard, who had by this time come down the Rhine as far as Lauterberg to defend a possible attack upon Alsace, knew certainly that the Danube, and not the Rhine, would be the field of war.

All this time it was guessed at Versailles, and thought possible by the French generals at the front, that the Danube was Marlborough's aim. But a guess was not good enough to risk Alsace upon.

By the time it was certain Marlborough was marching for the Danube—June 4th and 5th—Tallard's force was much further from the Elector of Bavaria than was Marlborough's, as a glance at the map will show. There was no chance then for heading Marlborough off, and the chief object of the English commander's strategy was accomplished. He had kept the enemy in doubt[3] as to his intentions up to the moment when his forces were safe from interference, and he could strike for the Danube quite unmolested.

Villeroy at once came south in person, and joined Tallard at Oberweidenthal. The two commanders met upon the 7th of June to confer upon the next move, but at this point appeared that capital element of delay which hampered the French

---

[2] As the French dispatch goes, 7500 men, every horse, and all the waggons, save 120, which had got into difficulties on the way; Fortescue's note suggesting that 1500 men only reached the Franco-Bavarians (vol. i. p. 42) is based on Quincy.

[3] It is, of course, an error to say, as is too often done in our school histories and the official accounts of our universities, that the French commanders had no idea of a march upon the Danube. A child could have seen that the march upon the Danube was one of the possible plans open to Marlborough, and Villeroy expressly mentions the alternative in his letter of the 30th of May. The whole point of Marlborough's manœuvres was to leave the enemy in doubt until the very last moment as to which of the three, the Danube, the Moselle, or Alsace, he would strike at; and to be well away upon the road to the former before the French had discovered his final decision.

forces throughout the campaign, namely, the necessity of consulting with the King at Versailles. The next day, the 8th, Tallard and Villeroy, who had gone back to their respective commands after their conference, sent separate reports to Versailles. It was not until the 12th that Louis answered, leaving the initiative with his generals at the front, but advising a strong offensive upon the Rhine in order to immobilise there a great portion of the enemy's forces.

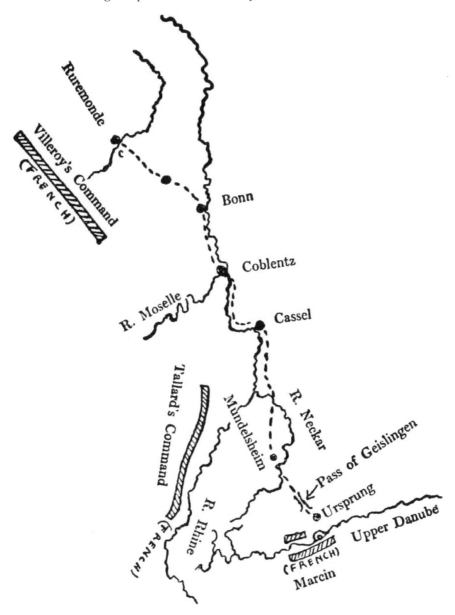

Map illustrating Marlborough's march to the Danube.

The advice was not unwise. It did, as a fact, immobilise Eugene for the moment, and kept him upon the Rhine for some weeks, but, as we shall see later, that General was able to escape when the worst pressure was put upon him, to cross the Black Forest with excellent secrecy and speed, and to effect his junction with Marlborough in time for the battle of Blenheim.

But, meanwhile, Baden had chased the Elector of Bavaria out of the Black Forest and down on to the Upper Danube. Marlborough might, at any moment, join hands with Baden. The Elector sent urgent requests for yet more reinforcements from the French, and Tallard, in a letter to Versailles of the 16th of June, advised the capture and possession of such points in the Black Forest as would give him free access across the mountains, the proper provisioning of his line of supply when he should cross them, and the accomplishment of full preparations for joining the Elector of Bavaria in a campaign upon the Upper Danube.

Let the day when the French court received this letter be noted, for the coincidence is curious. At the very moment when Tallard's letter reached Versailles, the 22nd of June, Marlborough was effecting his junction with Baden outside the gates of Ulm at Ursprung. The decision of Louis XIV., that Tallard should advance beyond the hills in force to the aid of the Elector, exactly coincides with the appearance of the English General upon the Danube, and it was on the 23rd of June, the morrow, that the King wrote to Villeroy the decisive letter recommending Tallard to cross over from Alsace towards Bavaria with forty battalions and fifty squadrons, say 25,000 men.

But this advance of Tallard's across the Black Forest and his final junction with the Elector and Marcin before the battle of Blenheim did not take place until after Marlborough had joined Baden and the march to the Danube was accomplished. It must therefore be dealt with in the next division, which is its proper place. For the moment we must return to Marlborough's advance upon the Danube, which we left at the point where he crossed the Neckar upon the 3rd and 4th of June. He had, as we have just seen, and by methods which we have reviewed, completely succeeded in saving the rest of his advance from interference.

Safe from pursuit, and with no further need for concealing his plan, Marlborough lingered in the neighbourhood of the Neckar, partly to effect a full concentration of his forces, partly to rest his cavalry. It was a week before he found himself at Mundelsheim, between Heilbron and Stuttgart, and at the foot of the range which still divided him from the basin of the Danube. Here Eugene, the author of the whole business, met Marlborough; between them the two men drew up the plans which were to lead to so momentous a result, and knitted in that same interview a friendship based upon the mutual recognition of genius, which was to determine seven years of war.

Upon the 13th of June these great captains met and conferred also with the Margrave, Louis of Baden, who commanded all the troops in the hills, and who was to be the third party to their plan. He was a man, cautious, but able, easily ruffled in his dignity, often foolishly jealous of another's power. He insisted that Marlborough and he should take command upon alternate days—he would not serve as second—and in all that followed, the personal relations between himself and Marlborough grew less and less cordial up to the eve of the great battle. His prudence and arrangement, however, his exact synchrony of movement and good hold over his troops, made Marlborough's decisions fruitful.

Upon the 14th of June the passage of Marlborough's column over the hills between the Rhine and the Danube began. Baden went back to the command of his army, which already lay in the plain of the Upper Danube, and awaited the arrival of Marlborough's command, and the junction of it with his own force before Ulm.

A heavy rain, drenched and bad roads, marked Marlborough's crossing of the range. It was not until the 20th that the cavalry reached the foot of the final ascent, but in two days the whole body had passed over. It was thus upon the 22nd of June that the junction between Marlborough and Baden was effected. From that day on their combined forces were prepared to operate as one army upon the plain of the Upper Danube. They stood joined at the gates of Ulm, and in their united force far superior to the Franco-Bavarians, who had but just escaped Baden's army, and who lay in the neighbourhood watching this fatal junction of their rivals.

I say, "who had but just escaped Baden's army," for it was part of the general plan (and a part most ably executed) that not only should the seat of war be brought into the valley of the Upper Danube by Marlborough's march to join Baden, but, as a preparation for this, that the army of the Elector, with his French allies under Marcin, should be driven eastward out of the mountains and cut off from the main French forces upon the Rhine.

This chasing of the Franco-Bavarians down on to the Danube and out of the Black Forest was begun just after the spirited piece of generalship by which Tallard had, as we have seen, reinforced the Elector of Bavaria in the middle of May. That rapid and brilliant piece of work had been effected only just in time. Hardly was it accomplished when Baden's force in the mountains marched, as part of Marlborough's general plan, against the Elector, with the object of forcing him back into the Danube valley at full speed.

It was on the 18th of May that the British regiments were crossing the Meuse, and the advance upon the Danube had begun.

It was on the 18th of May that Louis of Baden appeared at the head of his army in the Black Forest and initiated that separation of the Bavarian forces from the French which was a necessary part of the general plan we have spoken of. It was but a few hours since Tallard had stretched out his hand and passed the recruits and the provisions over to the Franco-Bavarian forces.

The Elector of Bavaria had with him certain French regiments, and Marshal Marcin was under his commands, while Marlborough's plan was still quite unknown. Therefore no large French force could apparently be spared from the valley of the Rhine to help the Elector in that of the Danube; the Duke of Baden could have things his own way against the lesser force opposed to him.

On the 19th he was advancing on Ober and Neder Ersasch. The Duke of Bavaria had evacuated these villages upon the 20th, and on the same night the Duke of

Baden reached Meidlingen. Pursuer and pursued were marching almost parallel, separated only by the little river of Villingen. Now and then they came so close that Baden's artillery could drop a shot into the hurrying ranks of the Elector.

On the 21st Baden was at Geisingen, threatening Tuttlingen. On the 23rd he had reached Stockach, and was pressing so hard that his van had actually come in contact with the rear of the Bavarians, a situation reminiscent of the Esla Bridge in Moore's retreat on Coruña.

The valley of the Danube opened out before the two opponents. The Elector found it possible to maintain his exhausted but rapid retreat, and, ten days later, he had escaped. For by the 3rd of June the Franco-Bavarian forces lay at Elchingen, the Duke of Baden was no nearer than Echingen, and the former was saved after a fortnight of very anxious going; but, though saved, they were now completely cut off for the moment from French reinforcement. Marlborough was approaching the hills; he would cross them in a few days. He would join Baden's army; and the moment Marlborough should have joined Baden, the Elector would be in peril of overwhelming adversaries.

We have seen how the plan matured. Three weeks after the Bavarian army's escape from the Black Forest, upon the 22nd of June, Marlborough's force had crossed the range and made one with Baden's before Ulm.

# PART IV

## THE SEVEN WEEKS—THE THREE PHASES

From the day when the Duke had appeared upon the southern side of the mountains, and was debouching into the plains of the Danube, to the day when he broke the French line at Blenheim, is just over seven weeks; to be accurate, it is seven weeks and three days. It was on the last Sunday but one of the month of June that he passed the mountains; it was upon the second Wednesday of August that he won his great victory.

These seven weeks divide themselves into three clear phases.

The first is the march of Marlborough and Baden upon Donauwörth and the capture of that city, which was the gate of Bavaria.

The second is the consequent invasion and ravaging of Bavaria, the weakening of the Elector, and his proposal to capitulate; the consequent precipitate advance of Tallard to the aid of the Elector, and the corresponding secret march of Eugene to help Marlborough.

The third occupies the last few days only: it is concerned with the manœuvres immediately preceding the battle, and especially with the junction of Marlborough and Eugene, which made the victory possible.

### THE FIRST PHASE

*From the junction of Marlborough and Baden to the fall of Donauwörth*

When the Duke of Marlborough had joined hands with the forces of Baden upon the 22nd of June 1704 his general plan was clear: the last of his infantry, under his brother Churchill, would at once effect their junction with the rest at Ursprung, and he and Baden had but to go forward.

His great march had been completely successful. He had eluded and confused his enemy. He was safe on the Danube watershed, and within a march of the river itself. The only enemies before him on this side of the hills were greatly inferior in number to his own and his ally's. His determination to carry the war into Bavaria could at once be carried into effect.

With this junction the first chapter in that large piece of strategy which may be called "the campaign of Blenheim" comes to an end.

Between the successful termination of his first effort, which was accomplished when he joined forces with Baden upon the Danube side of the watershed in the village of Ursprung, and the great battle by which Marlborough is chiefly remembered, there elapsed, I say, seven summer weeks. These seven weeks are divided into the three parts just distinguished.

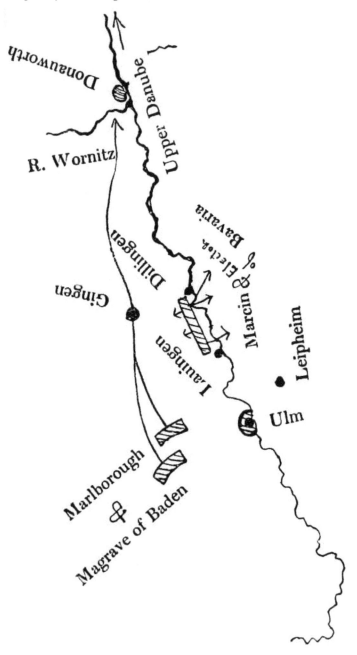

Map illustrating the march of Marlborough and Baden across Marcin's front from the neighbourhood of Ulm to Donauwörth.

In order to understand the strategy of each part of those seven weeks, we must first clearly grasp the field.

The accompanying map shows the elements of the situation.

East of the Black Forest lay open that upper valley of the Danube and its tributaries which was so difficult of access from the valley of the Rhine. In the hills to the north of the Danube, and one day's march from the town of Ulm, were now concentrated the forces of Marlborough and the Duke of Baden. They were advancing, ninety-six battalions strong, with two hundred and two squadrons and forty-eight guns: in all, say, somewhat less than 70,000 men.

At Ulm lay Marcin, and in touch with him, forming part of the same army, the Elector of Bavaria was camped somewhat further down the river, near Lauingen.

The combined forces of Marcin and the Elector of Bavaria numbered, all told, some 45,000 men, and their inferiority to the hostile armies, which had just effected their junction north of Ulm at Ursprung, was the determining factor in what immediately followed.

Marcin crossed the Danube to avoid so formidable a menace, and took up his next station behind the river at Leipheim, watching to see what Marlborough and the Duke of Baden would do. The Elector of Bavaria, in command of the bridge at Lauingen, stood fast, ready to retire behind the stream. The necessity of such a retreat was spared him. The object of his enemies was soon apparent by the direction their advance assumed.

For the immediate object of Marlborough and Baden was not an attack upon the inferior forces of the Elector and Marcin, but, for reasons that will presently be seen, the capture of Donauwörth, and their direct march upon Donauwörth took them well north of the Danube. On the 26th, therefore, Marcin thought it prudent to recross the Danube. He and the Elector joined forces on the north side of the Danube, and lay from Lauingen to Dillingen, commanding two bridges behind them for the crossing of the stream, and fairly entrenched upon their front. Meanwhile their enemies, the allies, passed north of them at Gingen. This situation endured for three days.[4]

---

[4] It is worthy of remark that the opportunity for victory which the weak forces under Marcin and the Elector of Bavaria offered at this moment to the superior forces of the allies would have led to an immediate attack of the last upon the first when, two generations later, war had developed into something more sudden and less formal, through the efforts of the Revolution.

Marlborough and the Duke of Baden, with their superior forces, would have attacked Marcin and the Elector had they been their own grandsons. Napoleon, finding himself in such a situation as Marlborough's a hundred years later, would certainly have fallen on the insufficient forces to his south, for it was known that reinforcements were coming over the Black Forest to save the Franco-Bavarian forces. To break up those forces before reinforcement should come was something which a sudden change of plan could have effected, but not even the genius of Marlborough was prepared, in his generation, for a movement necessitating so great a disturbance of calculations previously made. Donauwörth was his objective, and upon Donauwörth he marched, leaving intact this inferior hostile force which watched his advance from the south.

When it was apparent that the allied forces of the English general and the Duke of Baden intended to make themselves masters of Donauwörth (and the Elector of Bavaria could have no doubt of their intentions after the 29th of July, when their march eastward from Gingen was resumed), a Franco-Bavarian force was at once detached by him to defend that town, and it is necessary henceforward to understand why Donauwörth was of such importance to Marlborough's plan.

It was his intention to enter Bavaria so as to put a pressure upon the Elector, whose immediate and personal interests were bound up with the villages and towns of his possessions. The Elector could not afford to neglect the misfortunes of its civilian inhabitants, even for the ends of his own general strategy; still less could he sacrifice those subjects of his for the strategic advantage of the King of France and his marshal.

This Marlborough knew. To enter Bavaria, to occupy its towns (only one of which, Ingolstadt, was tolerably fortified), and if possible to take its capital, Munich, had been from its inception the whole business and strategic motive of his march to the Danube.

But if Marlborough desired to enter Bavaria, Donauwörth was the key to Bavaria from the side upon which he was approaching.

This word "key" is so often used in military history, without any explanation of it which may render it significant to the reader, that I will pause a moment to show *why* Donauwörth might properly be called in metaphor the "key" of Bavaria to one advancing from the north and west.

Bavaria could only be reached by a general coming as Marlborough came, on condition of his possessing and holding some crossing-place over the Danube, for Marlborough's supplies lay north of that river (principally at Nördlingen), and the passing of the enormous supply of an army over one narrow point, such as is a bridge over such an obstacle as a broad river, demands full security.

It will further be seen from the map that yet another obstacle, defending Southern Bavaria and its capital towards the west, as the Danube does towards the north, is the river Lech; a passage over this was therefore also of high importance to the Duke of Marlborough and his allies. Now, a man holding Donauwörth can cross both rivers at the same time unmolested, for they meet in its neighbourhood.

Further, Donauwörth was a town amply provisioned, full of warehouse room, and in general affording a good advanced base of supply for any army marching across the Danube. It afforded an opportunity for concentration of supplies, it contained waggons and horses and food. Supplies, it must be remembered, were the great difficulty of each of the two opposed forces, in this moving of great numbers of men east of the Black Forest, in a comparatively poor country, largely heath and forest, and ill populated.

No serious permanent defences, such as could delay the capture of the town, surrounded Donauwörth; but up above it lies a hill, called from its shape "the Schellenberg" or "Bell Hill." This hill is not isolated, but joins on the higher ground to its north by a sort of flat isthmus, which is level with the summit or nearly so.[5]

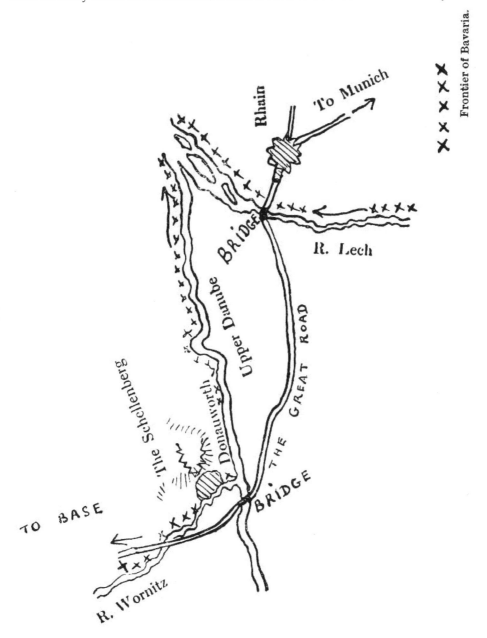

**Map showing how Donauwörth is the key of Bavaria from the North-West.**

The force which, on perceiving the Duke of Marlborough's intention of capturing Donauwörth, the Elector of Bavaria very rapidly detached to defend that

[5] As a fact, the advance along this "isthmus" on to the Schellenberg is slightly downhill, and against artillery of modern range and power the Schellenberg could not be held.

town, was under the command of Count d'Arco; it consisted of two regiments of cavalry and about 10,000 infantry (of whom a quarter were French). D'Arco had orders to entrench the hill above the town as rapidly as might be and to defend it from attack; for whoever held the Schellenberg was master of Donauwörth below. But the Elector could only spare eight guns for this purpose from his inferior forces.

Upon the 2nd of July, in the early morning, Marlborough, by one of those rapid movements which were a prime element in his continuous success, marched before dawn with something between seven and eight thousand infantry carefully chosen for the task and thirty-five squadrons of horse for the attack on the Schellenberg. It was Marlborough's alternate day of command.

With all his despatch, he could not arrive on the height of the hill nor attack its imperfect but rapidly completing works until the late afternoon. It is characteristic of his generalship that he risked an assault with this advance body of his without waiting for the main part of the army under the Duke of Baden to come up. With sixteen battalions only, of whom a third were British, he attempted to carry works behind which a force equal to his own in strength was posted. The risk was high, for he could hardly hope to carry the works with such a force, and all depended upon the main body coming up in time. There was but an hour or two of daylight left.

The check which Marlborough necessarily received in such an attempt incidentally gave proof of the excellent material of his troops. More than a third of these fell in the first furious and undecided hour. They failed to carry the works. They had already once begun to break and once again rallied, but had suffered no final dissolution under the ordeal—though it was both the first to which the men were subjected during this campaign, and probably also the most severe of any they were to endure.

Whether they, or indeed any other troops, could long have survived such conditions as an attempt to storm works against equal numbers is not open to proof; for, while the issue was still doubtful (but the advantage naturally with the force behind the trenches), the mass of the army under the Duke of Baden came up in good time upon the right (that is, from the side of the town), poured almost unopposed over the deserted earthworks of that side, and, five to one, overwhelmed the 12,000 Franco-Bavarians upon the hill.

After one of those short stubborn and futile attempts at resistance which such situations discover in all wars, the inevitable dissolution of d'Arco's command came before the darkness. It was utterly routed; and we may justly presume that not 4000—more probably but 3000—rejoined the army of Marcin and of the Elector of Bavaria.

The loss of the Schellenberg had cost Marlborough's enemies, whose forces were already gravely inferior to his own, eight guns and close upon one-fifth of their effective numbers. The Franco-Bavarians hurried south to entrench themselves under Augsburg, while Donauwörth, and with it the passage of the two great rivers and the entry into Bavaria, lay in the possession of Marlborough and his ally.

The balance of military and historical opinion will decide that Marlborough played for too high stakes in beginning the assault so late in the evening and with so small a force. But he was playing for speed, and he won the hazard.

It was a further reward of his daring that he could point after this first engagement to the fine quality of his British contingent.[6]

It was upon the evening of July the 2nd, then, that this capital position was stormed. It was upon the 5th that Marcin and the Elector lay hopeless and immobile before Augsburg, while their enemies entered a now defenceless Bavaria by its north-western gate. And this complete achievement of Marlborough's plan was but the end of the first phase in the campaign upon the Danube.

Meanwhile, a large French reinforcement under Tallard was already far up on its way from the Rhine, across the Black Forest, to join Marcin and the Elector of Bavaria and set back the tide of war, and, when it should have effected its junction with those who awaited it at Augsburg, to oppose to Marlborough and the Duke of Baden a total force greater than their own.

The French marshal, Tallard, was in command of the army thus rapidly approaching in relief of the Franco-Bavarians. His arrival, if he came without loss, disease, or mishap, promised a complete superiority over the English and their allies, unless, indeed, by some accident or stroke of genius, reinforcement should reach *them* also before the day of the battle.

This reinforcement, in the event, Marlborough *did* receive. He owed it, as we shall see, to the high talents of Prince Eugene; and it is upon the successful march of this general, his junction with Marlborough, and the consequent success of Blenheim, that the rest of the campaign turns.

We turn next, then, to follow the second phase of the seven weeks, which consists in Tallard's advance to join the Elector, and in Eugene's rapid parallel march, which brought him, just in time, to Marlborough's aid.

## THE SECOND PHASE

### *The Advance of Tallard*

To follow the second phase of the seven weeks, that is, the phase subsequent to the capture of the Schellenberg and the retirement of Marcin and the Elector of Bavaria on to Augsburg, it is necessary to hark back a little, and to trace from its origin that advance of Tallard's reinforcements which was to find on the field of Blenheim so disastrous a termination.

We shall see that in this second phase Tallard did indeed manage to effect his junction with the Elector and Marcin with singular despatch; that this junction compelled Marlborough and Baden to cease the ravaging of Bavaria upon which they had been engaged, and to join in closely watching the movement of the Franco-Bavarian forces, lest their own retreat or their line of supplies should be cut off

[6] Of seventeen officers of the Guards, twelve were hit; of the total British force at least a third fell; more than a third of these, again, were killed.

by that now large army.

The Schellenberg was stormed, as we have seen, on the 2nd of July.

Tallard, as we have also seen, had orders from Versailles, when Marlborough's plan of reaching the Danube was clear, to put himself in motion for an advance to the Elector's aid.

He moved at first with firmness and deliberation, determined to secure every post of his advance throughout the difficult hills, and thoroughly to provision his route. He crossed the Rhine upon July 1st, and during the very hours that, far to the east, the disaster of Donauwörth was in progress, he was assembling his forces upon the right bank of the river before beginning to secure his passage through the Black Forest. Upon the 4th he began his march over the hills.

A week later he was in the heart of the broken country at Hornberg, and on the 16th of July he had contained the garrison of Villingen, the principal stronghold which barred his route to the Danube, and which, did he leave it untaken, would jeopardise his provision and supply, the health and even the maintenance of his horses and men by the mountain road.

Upon the 18th he opened fire upon the town; but on the very day that the siege thus began he received from Marcin the whole story of the disaster of the Schellenberg, which had taken place a fortnight before, and a most urgent request for immediate reinforcement.

Tallard's deliberation, his attempt to secure the enemy's one stronghold upon the line of his passage across the hills, and amply to provision his advance, were fully justified. He knew nothing of the fall of Donauwörth. He believed himself to have full time for a properly organised march to join the Elector of Bavaria, and that meant the capture of Villingen. And the siege of that fortress had the further advantage that it compelled Eugene and his army to remain near the Rhine. Only at this late day, the 18th of July, did Tallard learn that the forces of Marlborough and of Baden had captured the crossing of the Danube and the Lech, and were pouring into Bavaria.

He should have known it earlier, but the despatch which bore him the information had miscarried.

Already, upon the 9th, Marcin had written from Augsburg a pressing letter to Tallard, bidding him neglect everything save an immediate march, and, ill provisioned as he was, and insecure as he would leave his communications, to hasten to the aid of the Elector. Marlborough and Baden (he wrote) had crossed the Danube and the Lech on the 5th and 6th of July. They were before Rhain; and when Rhain fell (as fall it must), all Bavaria would be at their mercy.

This letter Tallard never received.

Marcin was right. Rhain could not possibly hold out: none of the Bavarian strongholds except Ingolstadt were tolerably fortified. Rhain was destined to fall, and with its fall all Bavaria would be the prey of the allied generals.

The Elector, watching all this from just beyond the Lech, was in despair. He proposed to sue for terms unless immediate news of help from the French upon the Rhine should reach him. And if the Elector sued for terms and retired from the contest, France would be left alone to bear the whole weight of the European alliance: its forces would at once be released to act upon the Rhine, in Flanders, or wherever else they would.

When, upon the 14th, Marcin wrote that second letter to Tallard, telling him to neglect everything, to march forward at all costs, and to hasten to Bavaria's relief—the letter which Tallard did receive, and which came to him on the 18th of July, just as he was beginning the siege of Villingen—Rhain still held out; but, even as Tallard read the letter, Rhain had fallen, and the terrible business of the harrying of Bavaria had begun. For Baden and Marlborough proceeded to ravage the country, a cruel piece of work, which Marlborough believed necessary, because it was his supreme intention to bring such pressure to bear upon the Elector as might dissuade him from taking further part in the war.

The villages began to burn (one hundred and twenty were destroyed), the crops to be razed. The country was laid waste to the very walls of Munich, and that capital itself would have fallen had the Englishman and his imperial ally possessed a sufficient train to besiege it.

Tallard was still hesitating to abandon the siege of Villingen when, upon the 21st of July, came yet a *third* message from Marcin, which there was no denying. Tallard learnt from it of the fall of Rhain, of the ravaging of Bavaria, of the march of Marlborough and Baden upon Munich, of the crucial danger in which France lay of seeing the Elector of Bavaria abandon her cause.

Wholly insufficient as the provisioning of the route was, Marcin assured Tallard it was just enough to feed his men and horses during the dash eastwards; and, with all the regret and foreboding necessarily attached to leaving in his rear an unconquered fortress and marching in haste upon an insufficiently provided route, Tallard, on the next day, the 22nd, raised the siege of Villingen and risked his way across the mountains down to the valley of the Danube.

The move was undoubtedly necessary if the Bavarian alliance was to be saved, but it had to be accomplished in fatal haste.

Sickness broke out among Tallard's horses; his squadrons were reduced in a fashion that largely determined the ultimate issue at Blenheim.

His troops, ill fed and exhausted, marched upon wretched rations of bread and biscuit alone, and with that knowledge of insecurity behind them which the private soldier, though he can know so little of the general plan of any campaign, instinctively feels when he is taking part in an advance of doubtful omen.

A week later, upon the 29th of July, the army was in sight of Ulm. It found there but six thousand sacks of flour. It knew that it would find no sufficient provisionment in Augsburg at the end of its advance, yet advance it must unless the forces of Bavaria were to be lost to the cause of Louis XIV.

Five days later the junction was effected, and upon Monday the 4th of August the united armies of Tallard and the Elector of Bavaria faced, in the neighbourhood of Augsburg, the opposing armies of Marlborough and Baden upon the further side of the Lech.

In spite of the deplorable sickness and loss among his horse, the absence of remounts, the exhaustion of his men, the poor provisioning, and the insecurity of the line of supply behind him, Tallard could now present forces somewhat superior (counted by battalions and nominal squadrons)—far superior in artillery—to the forces of the allies.

Had this reluctant and tardy advance of Tallard's on the one hand, the ravaging of Bavaria by Baden and Marlborough on the other, between them constituted the whole of the second phase in the preliminaries of Blenheim, the result of the campaign might have been very different, in spite of the impoverished condition of the Franco-Bavarian army.

But a third element, of the utmost importance, must be added: the rapid, the secret, and the successful march of Eugene during these same days across the northern part of these same hills which the French had just traversed by their southern passes, and the debouching of that formidable captain with his admirably disciplined force, especially strong in cavalry, upon the upper valley of the Danube to reinforce Marlborough and to decide the war.

So long as Tallard proceeded, with soldierly method, to the proper affirmation of his line of advance and to the reduction of Villingen, Eugene had been pinned to the neighbourhood of the Rhine.

Would Eugene, when the siege of Villingen was raised, and when Tallard had been persuaded to that precipitous eastern move, go back to hold the line of the Rhine against the French forces there situated, or would he decide for the risk of detaching a large command, perhaps of leading it himself, and of joining Marlborough? That was the doubtful factor in Tallard's plans.

As in the case of Marlborough's own march to the Danube, either alternative was possible. The safer course for Eugene, and that one therefore which seemed in the eyes of his enemies the more probable, was for him to remain on the Rhine. But it was conceivable that he would run the risk of leading a force to the Danube; and did he so decide, the whole business of the French remaining on the Rhine was to discover his intention, the whole business of Eugene to hide it.

As in the case of Marlborough's march to the Danube, Eugene was led by a just instinct to gamble on the chance of the French army in Alsace not noting his move, and of the few troops he left opposite them upon the Rhine sufficing to screen his movements and to give the effect of much larger numbers. In other words, though his task in the coalition was to watch the central Rhine, he decided to take the risk of seeing the Rhine forced, and to march in aid of the English general whom he had himself summoned to Bavaria, with whose genius his own had such sympathy, and at whose side he was to accomplish the marvels of the next seven years.

Like Marlborough, he was successful in concealing his determination, but, with a smaller force than Marlborough's had been, he was able to be more successful still.

Villeroy, who commanded the French upon the Middle Rhine, was informed by numerous deserters and spies that Eugene, after the fall of Villingen, was at Radstadt, and intended detaching but two or three battalions at most from his lines upon the right bank of the Rhine, and these not, of course, for work upon the Danube, but only to cover Wurtemburg by garrisoning Rottweil.

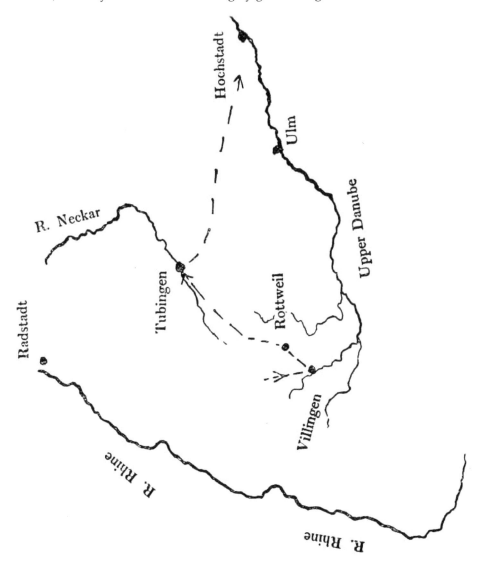

**Map showing Eugene's march on the Danube from the Black Forest.**

This information, coming though it did from many sources, was calculatedly false, and Eugene's movements, after the siege of Villingen had been raised, were arranged with a masterly penetration of his enemy's mind. A leisurely two days after the siege of Villingen was raised he entered that fortress, ordered the breaches to be repaired, and, in his every order and disposition, appeared determined to remain within the neighbourhood of the Upper Rhine. Nearly a week later he was careful to show himself at Rottweil, hardly a day's march away, apparently doing no more than cover Wurtemburg against a possible French attack from beyond the Rhine; and, so far as such leisure and immobility could testify to his intentions, he proclaimed his determination to remain in that neighbourhood, and in no way to preoccupy himself with what might be going on in the valley of the Upper Danube.

With due deliberation, he left eight battalions in Rottweil to garrison that place, posted seventeen upon his lines upon the Rhine, and himself openly proceeded—and that at no great speed—to march for the valley of the Neckar with 15,000 men.... Those 15,000 had been picked from his army with a particular care; nearly one-third were cavalry in the highest training, and the command, which seemed but one of three detachments all destined to operate upon the Rhine, was in fact a body specially chosen for a very different task. Eugene continued to proceed in this open fashion and slow as far as Tübingen....

It was many days since Tallard had begun his advance; many days since Villeroy, on the Rhine, had been watching the movements of Eugene; and during all these days that great general had done no more than assure his original positions with ample leisure, and to begin, with what was apparently a gross lack of concealment, a return by the Neckar round the north of the Black Forest to the Rhine valley.

Suddenly, from the moment of his reaching Tübingen, all this slow and patient work ceases. Eugene and his 15,000 abruptly disappear.

In place of the open march which all might follow, friend and foe alike, there is a void; in place of clear and reiterated information upon his unhurried movements, there is nothing but a fog, contradictory rumours, fantastic and ill-credited.

Never was a design better kept or concealed to a moment so near its accomplishment. When that design was accomplished, it was to determine, as we shall see in what follows, the whole issue of the campaign of Blenheim.

## THE THIRD PHASE

### *The Appearance of Eugene*

The third phase in the operations which led up to the battle of Blenheim is one of no more than nine days.

It stands distinct from all that went before, and must be regarded in history as a sort of little definite and enclosed preface to the great action. The distinctive character of this, the third phase, resides in the completion of the Franco-Bavarian force, its manœuvring in the presence of the enemy, and its finding itself unexpectedly confronted with the reinforcements of Eugene.

To seize the character of this third phase, the sketch map opposite must be referred to.

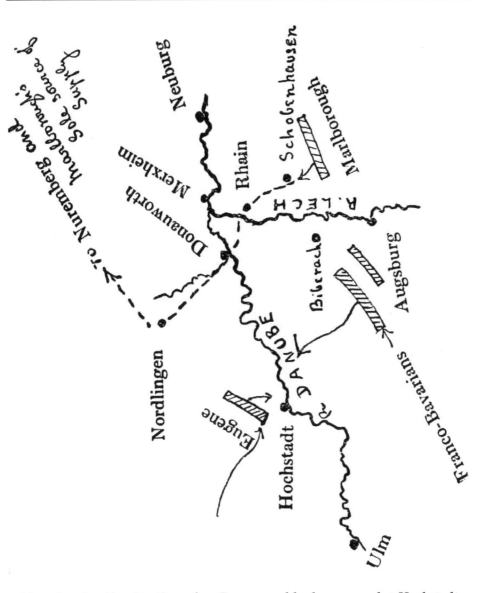

**Map showing the situation when Eugene suddenly appeared at Hochstadt, August 5-7, 1704.**

It is the 5th of August. Tallard has fully effected his junction with Marcin and the Elector of Bavaria, and the united Franco-Bavarian force lies in and to the east of Augsburg. On the opposite bank of the river Lech this force is watched by the army of Marlborough and Baden, which has been ravaging Bavaria. But Marlborough and Baden, though they have an advanced depot at Donauwörth, have their forward munitions and supplies far up northwards. Nördlingen is their advanced base, two days' marching beyond the Danube. A week away to the north Nuremberg contains their only large and permanent collection of stores. Marlborough and Baden are in perpetual difficulty for food, for ammunition, and for forage—especially for ammunition.

Since the whole object of Marlborough in marching to the Upper Danube was to embarrass in this new seat of war the alliance of the French and Bavarian forces, it is, conversely, the business of the French commander to get him out of the valley of the Upper Danube and restore the liberty of action of the French monarch and of his ally the Elector of Bavaria.

The surest way of getting Marlborough out of the Upper Danube is to threaten his line of supply. He will then be compelled to fall back northward upon his base. Further (though Tallard did not know it at the moment), there is present the very real difficulty of friction between the two commanders of the army opposing him. Marlborough and Baden are not getting on well together. If it were possible for Marlborough to persuade Baden to go off on some little expedition of his own, withdrawing but a few soldiers, Marlborough would be well content, and Marlborough is by far the more formidable of the two men. But though the opportunity for such a riddance of divided command is open, for Prince Louis of Baden is anxious to besiege Ingolstadt, Marlborough dares not weaken the combined forces, even by a few battalions, now that Tallard has effected his junction with the Elector and with Marcin, and that a formidable force is opposed to him.

These elements in the situation, once clearly seized, the sequel follows from them logically enough.

The above describes the situation on the 5th of August.

On the 6th, Wednesday, the united Franco-Bavarian force began its march northward towards the Danube, a march parallel with Marlborough's line of supply, and threatening that line all the way, ready to cut it when once the northern bank of the Danube was reached. Marlborough was compelled, in view of that march, to go back northward, step for step with his opponents. The artery that fed him was in danger, and everything else must be neglected.

In the evening of that Wednesday, August the 6th, Tallard and the Elector were at Biberach, Marlborough and Baden at Schobenhausen, which, as the map shows, lies also a day's march to the north from the last position these troops had held, and was on the way to the crossing of the Danube at Neuburg, as the Franco-Bavarians were on the way to the crossing of the same great river at Dillingen.

On the 7th there was no movement, but on the 8th, the Friday, as the Franco-Bavarian host approached the crossing of the Danube at Dillingen, their leader (if Tallard may be regarded as their leader—he was nominally under the orders of the Elector, but he was the marshal of Louis XIV.) heard suddenly that Eugene *had appeared at Hochstadt with thirty-nine squadrons and twenty battalions.*

The trick was done. The rapid and secret march of Eugene had been accomplished with complete success, and his force was within speaking distance of Marlborough's.

When the news came to the French camp, it was even there evident what a sudden transformation had come over the campaign; but to one who could see, as the historian sees, the moral condition of both forces, the event is more significant still.

A great commander, whose name was henceforth to be linked most closely with that of Marlborough's himself, was present upon the Upper Danube. He brought with him troops not only equivalent in number to a third of his colleague's existing forces, but trained under his high leadership, disciplined in his excellent school, and containing, what will prove essential to the fortunes of the coming battle, a very large proportion of cavalry. Further, the appearance of Eugene at this critical moment permitted Marlborough to rid himself of Louis of Baden, to despatch him to the siege of Ingolstadt in the heart of Bavaria, at once to be free of the clog which the slow decision and slow movements of that general burdened him with, to threaten the heart of the enemy's country by that general's departure on such a mission, and to unite himself and his forces with a man whose methods were after his own heart.

It is true that a minor problem lay before Eugene and Marlborough which must be solved before the great value of the junction they were about to effect could be taken advantage of. Their forces were still separated by the Danube: Marlborough lay a day's march to the south of it, and were he to cross the Danube at Neuburg he would be two days' march from Eugene. But each army was free to march towards the other, and all that their commanders had to decide was upon which side of the river the junction should be effected. Were the junction effected to the south—that is, were Eugene to cross the Danube and join Marlborough in Bavaria—Tallard, crossing the Danube at Dillingen, could strike at the great northern line of communications which conditioned all these movements. It was, therefore, the obvious move for Eugene and Marlborough to join upon the *northern* bank of the Danube, and to move upon and defend that all-important line of communications, point for point, as Tallard might threaten it.

It was on the 8th, the Friday, as I have said, that Eugene's presence was known both to Tallard and to Marlborough, for Eugene had ridden forward and met his colleague.

Upon the 9th, the Saturday, the French marched towards the bridge of Dillingen. Eugene, who was already on the way back to his army, returned to inform Marlborough of this, then rode westward again to his forces, and, while the French made their arrangements for crossing the river on the morrow, he busied himself in conducting his 15,000 eastward down the north bank of the Danube. Three thousand of Marlborough's cavalry went forward to meet him, and to begin that junction between the two forces which was to determine the day at Blenheim.

The next day, Sunday the 10th, the Franco-Bavarian army passed the river and lay in the position with which their forces had in the past been so familiar, the position from Lauingen to Dillingen which Marcin and the Elector had held when, six weeks before, Marlborough and Baden had passed across the Franco-Bavarian front to the north in their march upon Donauwörth and the Schellenberg.

On the same Sunday, the 10th, Marlborough had brought up his main force to

Rhain, within an hour of the Danube, and Eugene was drawing up his force at a safe distance from the French position north of the village of Münster, and behind the brook of Kessel, where that watercourse joins the Danube.

But, though junction with Marlborough was virtually effected, it must be effected actually before Eugene could think himself safe from that Franco-Bavarian force a day's march behind him, which was three times his own and more. His urgent messages to Marlborough led that commander to march up his men through the night. Before the dawn of August the 11th broke, Churchill, with twenty battalions, had crossed at Merxheim, and the whole army, marching in two columns, was upon the move—the right-hand column following Churchill to the bridge of Merxheim, the left-hand column crossing the Lech by the bridge of Rhain, to pass the Danube at Donauwörth. In the afternoon of that Monday the whole of Marlborough's command was passing the Wornitz, and long after sunset, following upon a march which had kept the major part of the great host afoot for more than twenty hours, Eugene and Marlborough were together at the head of 52,000 men, established in unison, and defending, with now no possibility of its interruption, the line of communications from the north.

Every historian of this great business has justly remarked the organisation and the patient genius of the man who made such a concentration possible under such conditions and in such a time, without appreciable loss, at hurried notice, and with a complete success.

It is a permanent example and masterpiece in that inglorious part of war, the function of transport and of marching orders, upon which strategy depends as surely as an army depends on food.

Fully accompanied by his artillery, Marlborough's force could not have accomplished the marvel that it did; yet even this arm was brought up, in the rear of the army, by the morning of Tuesday the 12th, and from that moment, given a sufficient repose, the whole great weapon under the two captains could act as one.

On that same morning, Tuesday the 12th, the Franco-Bavarian army under Tallard and the Elector were choosing out with some deliberation a camp so situated as to block any movement of their enemy up the valley of the Danube. The situation of the camp was designed to make this advance up the Danube so clearly impossible that nothing would be left but what the strategy of the last few days had imposed upon Marlborough, namely, a retreat upon his base northward, away from the Danube, towards Nördlingen. It was not imagined that the two commanders of the imperial forces would attack this Franco-Bavarian position, and so risk a general action; for by a retreat upon Nördlingen their continued existence as an army was assured, while an indecisive result would do them far more harm than it would do their opponents. Did Marlborough and Eugene force an action, it is doubtful whether Tallard had considered the alternative of refusing it.

At any rate, on this Tuesday, the 12th of August, Tallard and the Elector had no intention but to take up a position and camp which would make a retreat up the Danube impossible to Marlborough and Eugene; and certainly neither imagined that any attempt to force the camp would be made, since an alternative of retreat and complete safety was offered the enemy towards Nördlingen.

While the French fourriers were ordering the lines of the encampment—the tents stretching, the streets staking out—the English duke and Eugene overlooked the business from the church tower of Tapfheim and saw what Tallard designed. Between the main of their own forces and the camp which the Franco-Bavarians were pitching was a distance of about five miles. The location of each body was therefore perfectly well known to the other, and rarely have two great hosts lain in mutual presence for full twenty-four hours in so much doubt of an issue, in such exact opposition, and each with so complete an apprehension of his opponent's power.

At this point—let us say noon of Tuesday, August 12th—it is essential for us to dwell upon the character of such battles as that upon which Marlborough was already determined; for by the time he had seen the French disposition of their camp, the duke had determined upon forcing an action.

It is the characteristic of great captains that they live by and appreciate the heavy risk of war.

When they suffer defeat, history—which soldiers and those who love soldiers so rarely write—contemns the hardiness of their dispositions. When victory, that capricious gift, is granted them, history is but too prone to fall into an opposite error, and to see in their hardihood all of the calculating genius and none of the determined gambler.

Justice would rather demand that the great captain should be judged by the light in the eyes of his men, by the endurance under him of immense fatigues, by the exact accomplishment of one hundred separate things a day, each clearly designed and remembered, by his grasp of great sweeps of landscape, by his digestion of maps and horizons, and finally and particularly by this—that the great captain, whether he loses or he wins, *risks* well: he smells the adventure of war, and is the opposite of those who, whether in their fortunes or their bodies, chiefly seek security.

Judged by all these tests, John Churchill, Duke of Marlborough, was a supreme commander; and it is not the least part in our recognition of this, that the first and chief of the great actions upon which his fame reposes was an action essentially and typically hazardous, and one the disastrous loss of which was as probable as, or more probable than, the successful issue which it obtained.

He could not know the special factor of weakness in his opponent's cavalry; he was to misjudge the first element in the position when he broke his best infantry in the futile attack upon the village. But he was to benefit by those small, hidden, momentary things which determine great battles, and which make of soldiers, as of men who follow the sea, determined despisers of success, and as determined worshippers of the merit which may or may not attain it.

To have led his army as he had led it for now three months, to have designed the general plan that he had designed, and to have accomplished it; to have effected the splendid concentration but a few hours since upon the Kessel—these formed a work sufficient to deserve the reward of victory, Marlborough had the fortune not only to deserve, but to achieve.

The night of that Tuesday fell with no alarm upon the one side or upon the other. In the camp of Marlborough and of Eugene was the knowledge that the twin commanders had determined upon an action; in that of Tallard and the Elector the belief that it was more probable their opponents would follow the general rules of war, and fall back to recruit their supplies by the one route that was widely open to them.

Midnight passed. It was already the morning of Wednesday the 13th before the one had moved, or the other had guessed the nature of his enemy's plan.

It was moonless and pitch-dark, save for the dense white mist which, in the marshy lands of that river valley, accompanies the turn of the August night. This mist had risen and covered the plain. The little villages were asleep after their disturbance by the advent of so many armed men. The cockcrows of midnight were now well past when there was stir in Marlborough's camp, and from this moment, somewhere about two of the morning of Wednesday, August the 13th, the action of Blenheim begins.

# PART V

## THE ACTION

The field of Blenheim has changed in its physical aspect less than any other of the great battlefields of Europe during the two hundred years and more that have passed since Marlborough's victory.

He who visits to-day this quiet Bavarian corn-land, with its pious and happy peasantry, its modest wealth, and its contempt for haste and greed, sees, if he come in the same late summer of the year, just what the mounted parties saw who rode out upon that Wednesday before the eight columns of Marlborough and Eugene under the early morning.

Thus, approaching the field of Blenheim from the east, the view consists in a low and strangely regular line of closely-wooded hills to the right and northwards; southwards, and to the left, a mass of undergrowth, the low trees of the marshes, occasional gaps of rank herbage which make bright green patches interspersing the woodland, mark the wide and marshy course of the Danube, with its belt of alluvial soil and swamp on either side.

Between this stretch of damp river-ground to the south and the regular low wooded hills to the north lies a plain just lifted above the level of the river by such few feet as are sufficient to drain it and no more. Crossing this plain transversely, on their way to the Danube, ooze and trickle rather than run certain insignificant streams; each rises in the wooded hills to the north, falls southward, and in the length of a very few miles reaches the main river. These streams are found, as one goes up the great valley, at every mile or so. With one, the Nebel, we shall be particularly concerned, for during the action at Blenheim it formed the only slight obstacle separating the two armies. This plain, which in August is all stubble, is some three miles across, such a space separates the hills from the river, and that distance, or a trifle more, is the full length of the little muddy brooks which thus occasionally intersect it.

To the eye which takes in that landscape at a first glance, bare of crops and under a late summer sun, the plain seems quite even and undisturbed by any hollows or rolls of land. It is, in fact, like most such apparently simple terrains, slightly diversified: its diversity is enough to affect in some degree the disposition of soldiers, to afford in certain places occasional cover, and to permit of opportunities for defence.

But these variations from the flat are exceedingly slight. The hollow which the Nebel has made, for instance, is not noticed on foot or even in mechanical traction as one follows the main road which runs the whole length of the plain, though if one goes across country on foot, one notices the slight bank of a few feet separating the cultivated land from a narrow belt of rough grass, which is boggy in wet weather, and which, in varying breadth, accompanies the course of the stream.

The plain also, as might be expected, rises slightly from its low shelf just above the Danube swamps and meadows, to the base of the hills. Its ascent in its whole three miles of breadth is but sixty feet.

Over this level sweep of tilled land rise at intervals the spires of rare villages, round which scattered houses and gardens of the Bavarian sort—broad-eaved, flat-roofed, gay with flowers—are gathered. But for these few human groups there is no break in the general aspect of the quite open fields.

As might be expected, an interrupted chain of such villages marks the line of the great river from Donauwörth to Ulm, each standing just on the bank and edge of what for long was the flood-ground of the Danube, and is still in part unreclaimed marsh and water meadow. Each is distant a mile or two from its next fellow. Thus, nearest Donauwörth we have Münster, upon which the left of the allied army reposed when it lay in camp before the battle. Next in order come Tapfheim and Schwenningen, through which that army marched to the field. Further up-stream another group stretches beyond the Nebel, the hamlet of Sonderheim, the little town of Hochstadt, the village of Steinheim, etc.; and, in the middle of this line, at the point where the Nebel falls into the old bed of the Danube, is built that large village of *Blindheim*, which, under its English form of BLENHEIM, has given the action the name it bears in this country.

I say "the old bed of the Danube," for one feature, and one alone, in that countryside has changed in the two hundred years, though the change is not one which the eye can note as it surveys the plain, nor one which greatly affects the story of the action. This change is due to the straightening of the bed of the great river.

At the time when Blenheim was fought, the Danube wound in great loops, with numerous islands and backwaters complicating its course, and swung back and forth among the level swamps of its valley. It runs to-day in an artificial channel, which takes the average, as it were, of these variations, drains the flood-ground, and leaves the old bed in the form of stagnant, abandoned lengths of water or reeds, in which the traveller can trace the former vagaries of the river. Thus Blindheim, which stood just above the broad and hurrying water at the summit of one such loop, is now 800 yards away from the artificial trench which modern engineering has dug for the river. But the new channel has no effect upon the landscape to the eye. The floor on which the Danube runs is still a mass of undergrowth and weeds and grass, which marks off the cultivated land on the south, as it has been limited since men first ploughed.

I have said that the little slow and muddy streamlet called the Nebel must particularly meet with our attention, because it formed at the beginning of the action of Blenheim a central line dividing the two hosts, and round its course may be grouped the features of the terrain upon which the battle was contested.

*Blindheim*, or, as we always call it, *Blenheim*, lay, as we have seen, just above the bank of the Danube at the mouth of this stream. Following up the water (which is so insignificant that in most places a man can cross it unaided in summer), at the distance of about one mile, is the village of *Unterglauheim*, lying above the *left* bank, as Blenheim does above the right. Further on, another three-quarters of a mile up the *right* bank, is the village of *Oberglauheim*; and where the water dribbles in various small streams from the hills, and at their base, where the various tiny rivulets join to form the Nebel, at the edge of the woods, is *Schwennenbach*.

The tiny hamlet of *Weilheim* may be regarded as an appendix of this last or of Oberglauheim indifferently. It lies opposite the latter village, but on the further side of the stream, and about half a mile away.

Right behind Oberglauheim, at the base of the hills to the westward, and well away from the Nebel, is the larger village of *Lutzingen*.

These names, and that of the Nebel, are sufficient for us to retain as we follow the course of the battle, remembering as we do so that one good road, the road by which the allies marched in the morning to the field from Münster, and the road by which the Franco-Bavarian forces retreated after the defeat—the main road from Donauwörth to Ulm—traversed, and still traverses, the terrain in its whole length.[7]

It was at two in the morning of Wednesday the 13th of August that the allies broke camp and began their march westward towards the field of Blenheim.

That they intended to reach that field was not at first apparent. They might equally well have designed a retirement upon Nördlingen, and it was this that the commanders of the Franco-Bavarian army believed them to intend. The dense mist which covered the marshes of the river and the plain above clung to the soil long after sunrise. It was not until seven o'clock that the advancing columns of the enemy were observed from the French camp, distant about a mile away, and beginning to deploy in order to set themselves in line of battle. But, though they were then first seen, their arrival had been appreciated two hours before,[8] and the French line was already drawn up opposite them on the further bank of the Nebel as they deployed.[9]

The French order of battle is no longer to be found in the archives, though we can reconstruct it fairly enough, and in parts quite accurately, from the separate accounts of the action given by Tallard, by Marcin himself, by Eugene, and from English sources. The line of battle of the allies we possess in detail; and the reader can approach with a fair accuracy the dispositions of the two armies at the moment when the action began, though it must be understood that the full deployment of Marlborough and Eugene was not accomplished until after midday on account of the difficulty the latter commander found in posting his extreme right at the foot of the hills and in the woods of Schwennenbach; while it must be further

[7] The railway from Ulm to Donauwörth follows the line of this road exactly, and is almost the only modern feature upon the field.

[8] Mr Fortescue (vol. i. p. 436) writes as though this were not the case. He has overlooked Tallard's letter to the minister of war of the 4th of September.

[9] A small body was left at Unterglauheim, but withdrawn as the allies advanced; and outposts lay, of course, upon the line of Marlborough's advance, and fell back before it.

noted that the first shots of the battle sounded long before its main action began, that is, long before noon—for the French guns upon the front of their line opened at long range as early as nine o'clock, and continued a lively cannonade until, at half-past twelve, Eugene being at last ready, the first serious blows were delivered by the infantry.

All this we shall see in what followed. Meanwhile we must take a view of the two armies as they stood ranged for battle before linesman or cavalryman had moved.

The map on following page indicates in general terms the situation of the opposing forces.

The French stood upon the defensive upon the western bank of the Nebel. Their camp lay behind their line of battle, a stretch of tents nearly two miles long.

It is particularly to be noted that though, for the purpose of fighting this battle, they formed but one army, the two separate commands, that of the Elector (with Marcin) and that of Tallard, were separately treated and separately organised. The point is of importance if we are to understand the causes of their defeat, for it made reinforcement difficult, and put two loosely joined wings where a strong centre should have stood.

Tallard's command, thirty-six battalions and (nominally) forty-four squadrons, extended from Blindheim to the neighbourhood of Oberglauheim. Its real strength may be taken at about 16,000 to 18,000 infantry, and at the most 5200 cavalry; but of these last a great number could not be used as mounted men.

The village of Oberglauheim itself, and all that stretched to the left of it up the Nebel as far as the base of the hills, was occupied by the army of Marcin and the Elector of Bavaria. This force was forty-two battalions and eighty-three squadrons strong. The cavalry in this second army, the left of the whole force, had been less severely tried by disease, rapid marching, and ill provisionment than that of Tallard. We may reckon it, therefore, at its full or nearly its full strength, and say that Marcin and the Elector commanded over 20,000 men and close upon 10,000 horse. In a word, the total of the Franco-Bavarian forces, though we have no documents by which to estimate their exact numbers, may be regarded, from the indications we have of the losses of the cavalry, etc., as certainly more than fifty and certainly less than fifty-three thousand men, infantry and cavalry combined. To these we must add ninety guns, disposed along the whole front after the fashion of the time, and these under the general and separate command of Frézelière.[10]

This disposition of the guns in a chain along the whole front of the line the reader is begged especially to note.

_____

[10] Mr Fortescue gives the total force of cavalry under Marcin and the Elector at one hundred and eight squadrons and the infantry at forty-six battalions. The French official record gives forty-two battalions (not forty-six) and eighty-three squadrons in the place of one hundred and eight. Mr Fortescue gives no authority for his larger numbers; and, on the general principle that, in a contested action, each force knows best about its own organisation, I have followed these official records of the French as the most trustworthy.

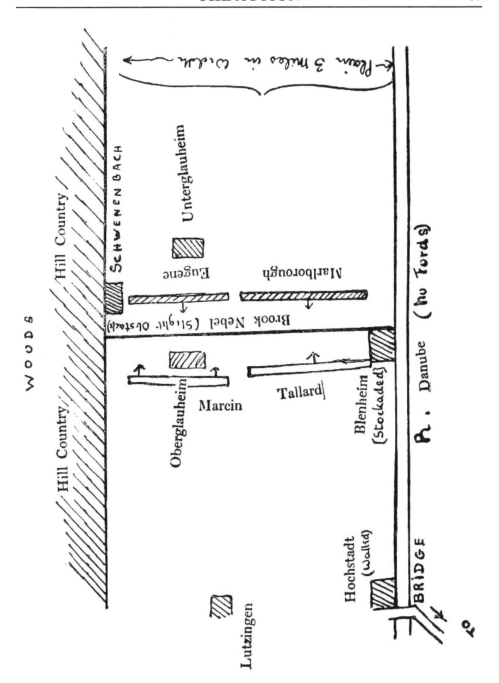

**The Elements of the Action of Blenheim.**

The particular dispositions of the Franco-Bavarian forces must now be seized, and to appreciate these let us first consider the importance of the village of Blenheim.

Blenheim, a large scattered village, with the characteristic Bavarian gardens round each house, lay so close to the course of the Danube as it then ran that there was no possibility of an enemy's force passing between it and the river. It formed a position easy to be defended, lying as it did on a slight crest above the brook Nebel, where that brook joined the main river.

Blenheim, therefore, if it were soundly held, blocked any attempt to turn the French line upon that side; but if it were carried by the enemy, that enemy would then be able to enfilade the whole French line, to take it in flank and to roll it up. Tallard, therefore, with perfect judgment, posted in the village a very strong force of his infantry. This force consisted at first of nine battalions, shortly after, by reinforcement, of sixteen battalions of foot, and further of four regiments of dragoons *dismounted*.[11]

Not content with throwing into Blenheim between 8000 and 10,000 men, Tallard placed behind the village and in its neighbourhood a further reserve of at least eleven battalions. Of his thirty-six battalions, therefore, only nine remained to support his cavalry over the whole of the open field between Blenheim and Oberglauheim, a distance of no less than 3500 yards. Consequently, this great gap had to be held in the main by his insufficient and depleted cavalry. Eight squadrons of these (of the red-coated sort called the Gendarmerie) formed the first section of this line, stretching from Blenheim to the neighbourhood of the main road and a little beyond it. Further along, towards Oberglauheim, another ten squadrons of cavalry were lined up to fill the rest of the gap. In a second line were ten more squadrons of cavalry under Silly; and the nine battalions of infantry remaining, when those in and near Blenheim had been subtracted, lay also in the second line, in support of the cavalry of the first line.

Such was Tallard's disposition, of which it was complained both at the time and afterwards that in putting nearly the whole of his infantry upon his right in the village of Blenheim and behind it he far too greatly weakened the great open gap between Blenheim and Oberglauheim. His chief misfortune was not, however, lack of judgment in this, but the character of the man who commanded the troops in Blenheim. This general officer, whose name was Clérambault, was of the sort to be relied upon when orders are strict and plain in their accomplishment: useless in an emergency; but it is only an emergency that proves the uselessness of this kind of man. The army of the Elector and Marcin, which continued the line, similarly disposed their considerable force of cavalry in front, along the banks of the stream; their infantry lay, in the main, in support of this line of horse and behind it; they had also filled Oberglauheim with a mass of infantry; but the disposition of this left half of the French line is of less interest to the general reader, for it held its own, and contributed to the defeat only in this, that it did not at the critical moment send reinforcements to Tallard upon the right.

---

[11] It is essential to note this point. Mr Fortescue talks of the dragoons "trotting" to "seal up the space between the village and the Danube." If they trotted it was as men trot in their boots, for they were on foot. The incident sufficiently proves the ravages which disease accompanying an insufficiently provided march had worked in Tallard's cavalry.

In general, then, we must see the long French line set out in two main bodies. That on the right, under Tallard, had far the greater part of its infantry within or in support of Blenheim,[12] while the cavalry, for the most part, stretched out over the open centre of the field, with Silly's ten squadrons and what was left of the infantry in reserve. That on the left, under Marcin and the Elector, had its far more numerous cavalry similarly disposed upon its front along the brook, most of its infantry behind, and a great number of these holding the village of Oberglauheim, with cavalry in front of them also. Along the whole line the ninety guns were disposed in a chain, as I have described.

Such being the disposition of the French troops, let us now turn to that of the Imperialists and their English and other allies under Eugene and Marlborough. These appeared within a mile of the French position by seven in the morning, and all that part of their left which lay between the river and the highroad was drawn up within long range of the French artillery somewhat before nine o'clock. But, as a glance at the map will show, their right had to march much further in order to come into line along the course of the Nebel, the course of which leans away from the line of Marlborough's advance. The difficulty of swampy land under the hills and of woods made the final disposition of the extreme left particularly tardy and tedious, nor was it fully drawn up until just after midday. During all the interval of three hours a brisk cannonade at long range had been proceeding from the guns in front of the French line—and, as nearly always the case with artillery before the modern quick-firer, was doing less damage than the gunners imagined.

When the allied line was finally formed its disposition was as follows:—

On the extreme left six columns of infantry, half of which consisted of British regiments.[13]

These stood immediately opposite the village of Blenheim, and were designed for that attack upon it which Marlborough, in his first intention, desired to make the decisive feature of the action.

Next, towards the main road, came four lines, two of infantry before and behind, and in the midst two parallel lines of cavalry, the foremost of which was

---

[12] Nearly all the English authorities and many of the French authorities speak of the whole twenty-seven battalions out of Tallard's thirty-six as being in Blenheim from the beginning of the action, and Mr Fortescue adds the picturesque, but erroneous, touch that "Marlborough" (before the action) "had probably counted every one of the twenty-seven battalions into it" (Blenheim).

This error is due to the fact that at the close of the battle there actually were twenty-seven battalions within the village, but they were not there at the beginning of the action; and Marlborough cannot, therefore, have "counted" them going in. The numbers, as I have said, were first nine battalions, with four regiments of dismounted dragoons; then, a little later, another seven, making sixteen; then, *much later*, and when the French were hard pressed, yet another *eleven*, lying as a reserve *behind* Blenheim, were called into the village by the incompetence of Clérambault who commanded in Blenheim. He should have sent them to help the centre—as will be seen in the sequel.

[13] 1st battalion Royal Scots; 1st battalion First Guards; 8th, 20th, 16th, 24th, and 10th Foot; 3rd battalion 23rd Royal Welsh, 21st Royal Scots Fusiliers.

British, and in which could be distinguished the mounting and horsemanship of the Scots Greys.[14]

Next again, to the north, and astraddle of the great road, lay the main force; this it will be remarked was drawn up precisely in front of that part in the long French line which was the weakest, and which indeed consisted of little more than the ten squadrons of horse which filled the gap between the Gendarmerie and Oberglauheim. This main force was also drawn up in four great lines; the first of infantry, the two next of cavalry, the rear of infantry: it contained no British troops, and, with the others already mentioned, formed Marlborough's command. All the rest, along the north and the east, along the left bank of the Nebel, from Willheim up into the woods, and the gorge at the source of the brook, was Eugene's command—not a third of the whole.

As to the total strength of the allied forces which we must attempt to estimate as we estimated that of the Franco-Bavarians, we know it accurately enough—it was some 52,000 men. The opposing hosts were therefore little different in numbers. But it is of great importance to note the disproportion of cavalry. In that of the Imperialists under Marlborough and Eugene, not only was the cavalry better mounted and free from the fatigue and disease that had ravaged Tallard's horses, but it was nearly double in number that of its opponents. On the other hand, the artillery of the allies was far inferior. Only sixty-six guns at the most[15] were opposed to the French ninety.

Blenheim, in the issue, turned out to be a cavalry battle—a battle won by cavalry, and its effect clinched by cavalry. The poor rôle played by the guns and the inability of the French to make use of their numerical superiority in this arm was a characteristic of the time, which had not yet learnt to use the cannon as a mobile weapon.

A general action is best understood if the reader is first told the main event, and later observes how the details of its progress fit in with that chief character of it.

The main event of the battle of Blenheim was simply this:—

Marlborough first thought to carry Blenheim: he failed. Having failed before the village of Blenheim, he determined to break through Tallard's left, which formed the centre of the French line, and was successful in doing so. By thus breaking through the centre of the French line, he isolated all Tallard's army upon the right, except such small portion of it as broke and fled from the field. The remainder crowded into the village of Blenheim, was contained, surrounded, and compelled to surrender. The undefeated left half of the French line was therefore compelled to retire, and did so through Lutzingen upon the Danube, crossing which river in hurried retreat, it fell back upon Ulm. In one conspectus, the position at the beginning of the action was this:—

---

[14] From one to three squadrons each of the 1st, 3rd, 5th, 6th, 17th Dragoon Guards, 5th Royal Irish Dragoons, and a squadron of the Scots Greys.

[15] This is the number given by Eugene. Fortescue (p. 436) and most English authorities give fifty-two.

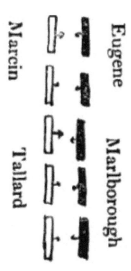

and at the end of it this:—

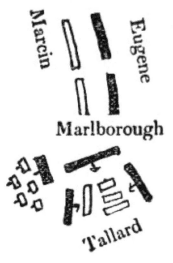

Now let us follow the details of the fight which brought about such a result.

First, at half-past twelve, when all was ready, came Marlborough's attack upon Blenheim.

We have seen some pages back how well advised was Tallard to treat Blenheim as the key of his position, and how thoroughly that large village, once properly furnished with troops and fortified with palisades, would guarantee his right. On that very account, Marlborough was determined to storm it; for if it fell, there would instantly follow upon its fall a complete victory. The whole French line would be turned.

It may be argued that Marlborough here attempted the impossible, but it must be remembered, in the first place, that he was by temperament a man of the offensive and of great risks. His first outstanding action, that of the Schellenberg, proved this, and proved it in his favour. Five years later, in one of his last actions, that of Malplaquet, this characteristic of his was to appear in his disfavour. At any rate, risk was in the temperament of the man, and it is a temperament which in warfare accounts for the greatest things.

First and last, some 10,000 men were employed against the one point of Blenheim; and the assault upon the village, though a failure, forms one of the noblest chapters in the history of British arms.

It was one o'clock of the afternoon when the serious part of the action opened by the two first lines of Marlborough's extreme left advancing under Lord Cutts to pass the Nebel, to cross the pasture beyond, and to force the palisades of the village. The movement across the stream was undertaken under a fire of grape from four guns posted upon a slight rise outside the village. Cutts' body crossed the brook in face of this opposition, re-formed under the bank beyond, left their Hessian contingent in shelter there as a reserve, while the British, who were the remainder of the body, advanced against the palisades.

The distance is one of about 150 yards. The Guards and the four regiments with them[16] came up through the long grass of the aftermath, Row at their head. Two-thirds of that short distance was passed in silence. The guns upon the slope beyond could not fire at a mark so close to their own troops behind the palisades. The English had orders not to waste a shot until they had carried the line of those palisades with the bayonet. The French behind the palisades reserved their fire.

It was one of those moments which the eighteenth century, with its amazingly disciplined professional armies, alone can furnish in all the history of war, an episode of which the Guards at Fontenoy were, a generation later, to afford the supreme example, and one depending on that perfection of restraint for which the English service was deservedly renowned. When a distance but a yard or two longer than a cricket pitch separated the advancing English from the palisades, the French volley crashed out. One man in three of the advancing line fell agonised or dead.

The British regiments, still obedient to Row's instructions, reserved their fire until their leader touched the woodwork with his sword. Then they volleyed, and having fired, wrestled with the palisades as though to drag them down by sheer force. Perhaps some few parties here and there pressed in through a gap, but as the English soldiers struggled thus, gripped and checked by the obstacle, the French fire poured in again was deadly; the British assault was broken, and fled in disorder over the little field to the watercourse. As it fled, the Gendarmerie charged it in flank, captured the colours of the 21st, were repelled again by the Hessians in reserve (who recaptured the flag), and the first fierce moment of the battle was over.

One-third of Cutts' command had been concerned in this first failure against Blenheim village. Two-thirds remained to turn that failure into a success. But be-

---

[16] The 10th, 21st, 23rd, and 24th.

fore this second two-thirds was launched, there took place an episode in the battle, not conspicuously noted at the time, and given a minor importance in all accounts save Tallard's own. It was significant in the extreme.

As Cutts' broken first line was passing out of range and was effecting its retirement after the first disorder, and after the Hessians had repelled the first and partial cavalry charge of the French, the Gendarmerie, eight squadrons strong, prepared to charge again as a whole. They came upon the English before these had regained safety. Cutts naturally begged for cavalry to meet this cavalry danger, and Lumley sent five British squadrons to cross the stream and check the French charge. The English horse came to the further bank after some little difficulty with the mud of the sluggish stream, which difficulty has been exaggerated, and in no way affected the significance of what followed.[17]

For what followed was the singular sight of eight French squadrons charging down a slope against only five, those five cramped in the hollow near a stream bed, and yet succeeding in receiving the shock of the charge of numbers so greatly superior, and, so far from yielding, breaking the offensive of their opponents into a confusion.

I repeat, it was but an episode, one that took place early in the day, and apparently of no weight. But, in a general historical view of the battle, it is of the first importance, for it showed what different stuff the opposed cavalries were made of, and that the allied army, which was already numerically the superior in cavalry—nearly double its opponents—had also better mounts, better riders, and a better discipline in that arm. A universal observer, seeing this one early detail in the battle of Blenheim, might have prophesied that the action would be a cavalry action as a whole, and that the cavalry of Marlborough would decide it.

I left Cutts prepared to launch the remaining two-thirds of his force at Blenheim village, in the hope of accomplishing what the first third had failed to do.

The whole combined body which the French had estimated at 10,000 men, and which seems to have been at least of some 8000, surged up in the second attempt against the palisades of the village. Part of that line and many of the outer gardens were carried, but the attack could not be driven home. It was, perhaps, at this moment that Tallard sent in those extra men which raised the French battalions in Blenheim from nine to sixteen, and gave the defenders, behind their walls, a force equal to the attackers. At any rate, the main attack was thrust back as the first had been, and the great corps of men, huddled, confused, rallied here and there as best they could be, broke from before the village.

The loss was terrible, and Marlborough having failed, not only failed, but saw that he had failed. It was his salvation. His subordinates would have returned to the fruitless attack with troops already shaken and dreading the ground. Marlbor-

[17] For some reason or other, the exaggeration of this feature—the marshiness of the banks of the Nebel—mars many an English account of the action. The Nebel, of course, was something of an obstacle, slight as it was, and in places the meadows on its bank widen out and are soft even in the dry weather which had as a whole distinguished the three weeks before Blenheim. But the crossing of that obstacle by the cavalry was nothing in the story of the battle. It was what the cavalry did *after they crossed* that counted.

ough ordered a false attack to be kept up from the further bank, upon the village, and, with that elasticity of command which is the prime factor of tactical success, and which commonly distinguishes youth rather than middle age in a general, turned all his efforts upon the centre.[18]

Here the main road crosses the Nebel by a stone bridge. Four other bridges had been thrown across at other points between this stone bridge and Unterglauheim. By these the infantry were crossing, which infantry, it will be remembered (and my frontispiece shows it), stood as to their first line in front of the cavalry in the main central body. This almost undisputed passage of the Nebel would not have been possible had not the distance between Blenheim and Oberglauheim been what it was. The gap was great, the French line defending it too thin, and the possibility of a cross fire defending the centre was eliminated by the width of that centre.

Even as it was, the passage of the Nebel led to one very difficult moment which might by accident or genius have turned the whole action in favour of the French; and in connection with this episode it must be remembered that the French commanders asserted that the passage of the Nebel was no success on the part of their enemy, but was deliberately permitted to that enemy in order that he might be overwhelmed upon the opposing slope, with the marshy stream behind him, when the time for a counter-attack should come.

The moment came when the greater part of Marlborough's cavalry had crossed, but before they had fully formed upon the further bank. While they were still in the disorder of forming, the French cavalry upon their left—that is, between the main road and Blenheim—charged down the slight slope, and something like a dismemberment of the whole of Marlborough's mounted line began. It was checked for a moment by the fire of the British infantry, during which check Marlborough brought over certain Danish and Hanoverian squadrons which had remained upon the further bank. But the French charged again, and though infantry of Marlborough's which was pouring over the stream up beyond the stone bridge came up in time to prevent a complete break down, the moment was critical in the extreme. All Marlborough's centre was pressed and shaken; a further spurt against it and it would break.

It was such a moment as commanders of rapid decision and quick eye have always seized; and if it be asked how Tallard should have seized it, the answer is that there were French guns to mass, there was French infantry in Blenheim unused, and more in reserve behind Blenheim wholly useless. There were the ten squadrons of Tallard's second line of cavalry under Silly, a couple of hundred yards away, to be summoned in a few moments.

Rapid decision and keen sight of this sort would have done the business; but Tallard was slow of perception; an excellent strategist, but short-sighted and a great gentleman; one, moreover, who had advanced by favour rather than by intrigue. He lost the moment.

Marlborough's cavalry managed to form, struggling beyond the brook, and the last final phase of the action was at hand—for Marlborough's cavalry would

[18] Marlborough was at this moment fifty-four years and two months old.

reiterate that general lesson which the whole battle teaches, to wit, that the horse of the allies was not only far stronger numerically, but far better trained than the French cavalry before them, and, with equal chances, must destroy it. Tallard, by missing his moment, had permitted those equal chances to be restored. Even so, yet one other last accident favoured the French. The hour was about five, or rather later in the mid-afternoon. In order to be able to form his cavalry beyond the Nebel, Marlborough wanted to have a clear right flank, and with that object he had launched from 6000 to 7000 Hanoverians against Oberglauheim. The excellent infantry of Blainville, less in numbers, emerged from the village, threw the Hanoverians into gross disorder, and captured their commander. At this point there was beginning to be a rout. This new French success, properly followed up, would again have had a chance to break the allied centre at its weakest point, just at the link where Marlborough joined on to Eugene.

Marcin, inferior as was his command, gripped the opportunity, sent cavalry at once to Oberglauheim, and that cavalry charged. But here the greatness of Marlborough as a personal commander suddenly appeared. He seized the whole character of the moment in a way that Tallard on his first chance had wholly failed to do. He put himself in person at the head of the Danish brigade that lay in reserve, brought it across the rivulet, and came just in time to take the charge of the French cavalry. Even as that charge was preparing, Marlborough sent to Eugene for cavalry at the gallop. He (Marlborough) must hold fast with his Danes against the French horse—five minutes, ten, fifteen at the most—till help should come from the right.

Here, again, another factor in the success of the day appeared—that Eugene and Marlborough understood each other.

Eugene had just suffered a sharp check upon the extreme right; he was re-forming for a new attack when he got Marlborough's message. Without the loss of a moment in weighing his own immediate necessities, he sent Fugger thundering off, and Fugger, with the imperial cuirassiers, came galloping full speed upon Marlborough's right flank just as the French charge was at its hardest pressure upon the Danish line. He took that French charge in flank, broke its impetus, permitted the Danish infantry to hold their own, and so compelled the French horse to fall back; within a quarter of an hour from its inception the peril of a breach in Marlborough and Eugene's centre was thus dissolved.

Here, then, is yet another incident in the battle, which shows not only on which side rapidity of perception lay, but also on which side lay sympathy between commanders, and, most important of all, the discipline and material eminence of the dominating arm.

It was now nearly six o'clock, and the August sun was red and low in the face of the English General. The French line still stood intact before him.

Marlborough's first great effort against Blenheim had disastrously failed all during the earlier afternoon; he had but just escaped a terrible danger, and had but barely been saved, by Eugene's promptitude in reinforcement, from seeing his line cut in two. Nevertheless, he was the master of the little daylight that remained. His cavalry, and indeed nearly all his troops, were now formed beyond the Nebel; he had the mass of his forces now all gathered opposite the weakest part of the French line. It was his business to pierce that line and to conquer.

As he advanced upon it, the French infantry, then stationed over the long evening shadows of the slope, though there deplorably few in numbers, met his advance by so accurate a fire that his own line for a moment yielded. Even then the day might have been retrieved if the French cavalry under Tallard's command had been capable of a charge. To charge—if we may trust the commander's record—they received a clear order. As a point of fact, charge they did not. A failure to comprehend, a tardy delivery of the dispatch, fatigue, or error was to blame—we have no grounds on which to base a decision. There was a discharge of musketry from the saddle, an abortive attempt to go forward, which in a few minutes was no more an attempt but a complete failure, and in a few more minutes not a failure but a rout. The words of Tallard himself, who saw that almost incredible thing, and who writes as an eye-witness, are sufficiently poignant. They are these:—

"I saw one instant in which the battle was won if the cavalry had not turned and abandoned the Line."

What happened was that the incipient, doubtful, and confused French charge had broken before a vigorous and united counter-charge of Marlborough's cavalry: the French horse backed, turned, bunched, fell into a panic; and when the mass of their cavalry had fled in that panic, the French centre, that is, the thin line of infantry still standing there, were ridden through and destroyed.

They lay in heaps of dead or wounded, cut down with the sword, for the most part unbroken in formation, their feet eastward whence the charge had come, and their faces to the sky. Over and beyond those corpses rode the full weight of Marlborough's cavalry, right through Tallard's left, which was the centre of the French line, while Tallard vainly called for troops to come out of Blenheim and check the fury, and as vainly sent for reinforcements to come from Marcin on the left, which should try and dam the flood that was now pouring through the bulwark of his ranks. On the left, Marcin heard too late. As to the messenger to Blenheim on the right he was taken prisoner; Tallard himself, hastening to that village, was taken prisoner in turn.

What followed, at once something inevitable and picturesque, must not be too extended in description for the purpose of a purely military recital. The centre being pierced, while the left under Marcin and the Elector still held its own against Eugene, the right, that is, the huddled battalions—now twenty-seven—within Blenheim village, and the four mounted regiments of dragoons therein, were the necessary victims of the victory. The piercing of the centre had cut them off from all aid. They were surrounded and summoned to surrender.

Clérambault, their commander, had already drowned himself in despair, or had been drowned in a deplorable attempt at flight—at any rate, was dead.

Blausac, an honest man, the second in command, refused to surrender. British cavalry rode round to prevent all egress from the village upon its western side. Churchill brought up the mass of Marlborough's infantry. Upon the side towards the Danube the churchyard was stormed and held. Still Blausac would not ask for terms.

## PLATE II. THE BATTLE OF BLENHEIM.

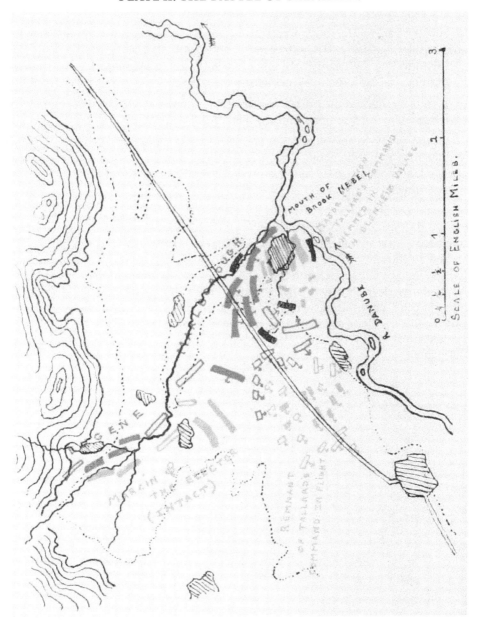

*To face page 59.*

It looked for a moment, under the setting sun of that fatal day, as though the 11,000 thus isolated within the streets of Blenheim would be massacred for mere glory, for Blausac was still obstinate. A subordinate officer, who saw that all was lost, harangued the troops into surrender, and the last business of the great battle was over.

As darkness gathered, the undefeated left under Marcin and the Elector—the half now alone surviving out of the whole host, the other half or limb being quite destroyed or surrendered—retreated with such few prisoners and such few colours as they had taken. They retreated hastily with all their train and their artillery, abandoning their camp, of course, and all through the night poured towards the Danube and built their bridges across the stream.

Darkness checked the pursuit. Some few remnants of Tallard's escaped to join the retreat. The rest were prisoners or dead.

Of the fifty odd thousand men and ninety guns that had marshalled twelve hours before along the bank of the Nebel, 12,000 men had fallen, 11,000 had surrendered, and one-third of the pieces were in the hands of the enemy.

The political consequences of this great day were more considerable by far than was even its character of a military success. It was the first great defeat which marked the turn of the tide against Louis XIV. It was the first great victory which stamped upon the conscience of Europe the genius of Marlborough. It wholly destroyed all those plans, of which the last two years had been full, for an advance upon Vienna by the French and Bavarian forces. It utterly cleared the valley of the Danube; it began to throw the Bourbons upon the defensive at last. It crushed the hopes of the Hungarian insurrection. It opened that series of successes which we couple with the names of Marlborough and Eugene, and which were not to be checked until, five years later, the French defence recovered its stubbornness at Malplaquet.


**FINIS.**

Lector House believes that a society develops through a two-fold approach of continuous learning and adaptation, which is derived from the study of classic literary works spread across the historic timeline of literature records. Therefore, we aim at reviving, repairing and redeveloping all those inaccessible or damaged but historically as well as culturally important literature across subjects so that the future generations may have an opportunity to study and learn from past works to embark upon a journey of creating a better future.

This book is a result of an effort made by Lector House towards making a contribution to the preservation and repair of original ancient works which might hold historical significance to the approach of continuous learning across subjects.

**HAPPY READING & LEARNING!**

**LECTOR HOUSE LLP**
E-MAIL: lectorpublishing@gmail.com

9 789390 387991

Ingram Content Group UK Ltd.
Milton Keynes UK
UKHW041839140423
420106UK00023B/106